THE HOUSE OF ISLÂM

THE HOUSE OF ISLÂM

MARMADUKE WILLIAM PICKTHALL

GYAN

Published by

Gyan Publishing House
5, Ansari Road
Daryaganj, New Delhi-110002
Phone: 011-47034999, 9811692060
E-mail: books@gyanbooks.com

Distribution Network
gyanbooks.com
India, USA, Canada, UK, Australia

ISBN: 978-93-7414-343-8 (PB)

First Published, 1906

2nd Impression 2026

Printed at: Gyan Press, Delhi.

THE HOUSE OF ISLÂM
Author: MARMADUKE WILLIAM PICKTHALL

THE HOUSE OF ISLÂM

THE HOUSE OF ISLÂM

BY

MARMADUKE PICKTHALL

"Man prays for Evil as he prays for Good, for man is unthinking."
—ALCORAN.

D. APPLETON AND COMPANY
NEW YORK MCMVI

THE HOUSE OF ISLÂM

INTRODUCTION

IN the reign of the Sultàn Abdul Mejìd Khan, upon termination of the war with Muscovy, a multitude of faithful Georgians and Circassians chose to cast themselves, their women and children, upon the bounty of the Padishah rather than endure the yoke of an infidel conqueror. They begged but leave to settle in some part of the Sultàn's dominions, to dwell in peace among true believers in obedience to the law of God, as transmitted to Muhammed, His Apostle. But their spokesmen had fierce eyes, and, when a little emphasis seemed called for, each clutched quite naturally at the dagger in his sash.

The Sultàn's advisers—black-coated, red-capped Othmanlis of the eyes that see but never look—noted this slight discrepancy while placidly telling their beads. There were lawless spots in the empire. On the confines of Esh-Shâm, for example, the peasants paid tax to the chiefs of the desert rather than to the lawful tithe farmer. There was a place with work in the world for men both loyal and warlike.

The Sultàn Abdul Mejìd heard those exiles. He clothed them in the mantle of his grace. Lands were granted in a far province, rights and privileges were conferred upon them. Letters written under the Tûghra made it a duty for all men to do them honor. And to prevent untoward collision with the old inhabitants, one Milhem Bey, a native of that country, was appointed to overlook the settlement and quell the disputes which were sure to arise at the outset.

Many days after the Circassians had set sail for their new land, one hot afternoon, this Milhem took boat at Tufana, down by the bridge, and went to visit his brother, a young doctor of the religion, who dwelt by the shore of Asia. As his caique shot forth into the strait, the coasts of Europe opened like a scroll. Fat domes and slender minarets rose up white from out dark cypress groves on the hill of Istânbûl. Heaped Ghalata and straggling Pera gathered beauty as their forms receded. The song of waters, with the pleasant sense of gliding, soothed Milhem. He closed his eyes upon the shining prospect, while he said in his soul:

"It is well. . . . Yet not altogether well. After fifteen years of obeisance, now at last I am lord of something—a small thing, but earnest of more to come. That is good. Praise to Allah, I am blest in that! . . . But it has taken long to reach this little eminence, and has cost me—Merciful Allah!—how much money! My patrimony is all but spent. And this post is not worth the trouble unless as a step to something finer. A few rock-scraping fellahìn, a few wild-beast Circassians. . . . What profit, O Lord, in such a government? After six months or eight I shall return. Then, it may be, they will speak to me of a pashalik. Where—Allah pity!—can I touch the price of a pashalik? Without money I can go no farther. If Shems-ud-dìn, my brother, will not help me, I must borrow of the infidel. O Shems-ud-dìn! O my soul! Allah knows it has been my sin to neglect thee. How long since I embraced thee, O my dear!"

The boat came to land at a point where a huddle of colored dwellings on the sea's brink and a mosque with needle-pointed minarets cast a shimmer on the smooth water. Milhem clambered out on to a landing stage and started to climb a path through orchards which led to his brother's house.

The Sheykh Shems-ud-dìn sat under a tree enjoying the view, across the strait, of the imperial city, when he was struck by the apparition of a white sunshade slowly bobbing up the path from the shore. Another minute and he sprang to his feet, crying, "Thanks to Allah!" With eyes alight, he ran to kiss his brother.

"They told me thou wast gone," he said, as he led him to the carpet under the tree. "But my heart informed me that they lied. Thou wouldst never have gone without my peace on thee. I am glad they lied who told me thou wast gone."

"Of a surety they lied," chuckled Milhem. "Everyone thought I should travel with those wild beasts. Only this morning one of the greatest called me laggard for remaining behind. Hear my answer! I said: 'O my lord, had I journeyed with the colonists, I had surely been a party to their quarrels as they arose. With your Grace's permission, let the quarrels first arise that I, coming as a stranger, may judge impartially with whom the right. Moreover,' I said, 'may it please your Highness, I would set my house in order ere I go. And your Excellency's self will admit that the city Istâna is mistress of more charm than the desert possesses.' I tell thee, he laughed, that great one; he laughed immoderately and praised my understanding. Men begin to perceive that Milhem Bey is not foolish. In sh' Allah he will be Milhem Pasha some day."

"In sh' Allah!" echoed Shems-ud-dìn vaguely.

"But a province costs much money!" sighed Milhem, at the same time darting a sharp glance at his brother's face.

The stupid had not heard. There he sat, fingering his great black beard, and gazing with his great brown eyes, full and wistful as a gazelle's, over the cypress tops of an adjacent cemetery, over the blue strait, to the crowding minarets of the city.

"Am I here to watch thee dreaming?" said Milhem tartly. "Art in love, or what ails thee?"

Shems-ud-dìn turned to him with a smile.

"Love, saidst thou? I have not loved these many days, since the death of one I loved truly. She whom I have now is but for appearance, lest neighbors should deem me disreputable, living alone. . . . I do but think, O my brother! I think, by Allah's leave, I go with thee."

Milhem flung up his hands and eyes to heaven.

"What a fancy!" he cried, affrighted. "May Allah heal thee of it quickly."

"Mock me not, O beloved!" pleaded Shems-ud-dìn. "Whom love I in the world like thee? While thou wast absent fighting in the holy wars, had my soul peace? And since then, seeing thee so seldom, have I been content? I adjure thee, by our love of old, gainsay me not in this matter!"

Launched upon a favorite theme, he continued in this strain of deep affection a great while.

Milhem answered not a word. Profoundly moved, he plucked up the grass near him by the roots, snuffling to keep from tears. At last, able to bear it no longer, he rose abruptly and took his leave with broken words of blessing and praise to God. Not until his boat danced midway across the path of darkening water, and the minarets of the sovereign city, aloft in the sunset, seemed spears of a phantom host uplifted, threatening, did he remember his purpose in the visit.

On the morrow, before noon, he found his way to the street of sweet odors, where Shems-ud-dìn had a shop which it was his custom to visit on that day of each week for the purpose of taking account with his steward. This morning Shems-ud-dìn was not alone. Two old men sat with him in the inner gloom, beyond where a group of women chaffered with the salesman. They were sheykhs renowned through all the world for their learning and piety, stern foes to innovation, for whom a time-serving official was an unclean beast.

Milhem bowed low before those holy ones, and blessed the lucky day.

After seats had been resumed, Shems-ud-dìn observed:

"I was telling these, my friends, of the journey I purpose to make. And they have honored me with a mission. . . ."

But Milhem stopped his ears, crying: "Think not of it, I beseech thee, O my brother! I come on purpose to restrain thee. With the permission of these reverend ones, thy thought to go with me is not of wisdom. Does a man right to quarrel with the part allotted? Behold thee here in great honor, with such friends about thee; yet not content! Thou must needs embark upon a venture—very perilous, very tiresome—whereunto no one calls thee. Do not so, O my brother, for the sin is great!"

"Once upon a time Eblìs himself met an angel from Allah, and, looking earnestly upon his face, observed, 'Sin not, I entreat thee,'" said one of the two old doctors in a manner of abstruse meditation.

Milhem bit his lips. He said, "Who am I to discuss what is right with the law's exponents? Yet, now and then, in my chamber, I give thought to these high matters. And it has seemed, to my little understanding, a sin that my brother should wander from a road so clear before him."

"By my beard, I see not the harm!" said the sheykh who had before spoken. "Why should not our friend, the learned Shems-ud-dìn, revisit his native land, a land of true belief? In sh' Allah, he will enjoy himself there. . . . But perhaps our lord the Bey would go alone. Two eyes of truth fixed constantly upon him embarrass the statesman."

"Which is only to say: 'He would keep his master's counsel.' Allah witness, I have no desire save for my brother's welfare."

"That is known for certain," cried Shems-ud-dìn heartily. "But fear not for me. I go gladly."

Milhem shrugged his shoulders. As soon as coffee had been served he took his departure. Where was the use in staying longer? These dotards showed no intention of moving, and he would not mention his need in their cold hearing.

At a later hour he returned that way, and, seeing Shems-ud-dìn alone in the depths of the shop, ran in and, stooping, kissed the hem of his robe. Through eagerness to convince, he magnified his want a hundredfold. By Allah, by the admirable Koràn, he had spent all his inheritance—had sown it rather, hoping to reap a rich crop of honor. His last para had gone to procure this beggarly appointment of governor over sundry wild beasts. On his return, if Allah kept him alive, he would have the offer of a wilâyet. Where in the world could he touch the price of a wilâyet? Rather than borrow of an Armenian or other usurious infidel, he would beg in the gate of one of the mosques; he had not yet decided which. He was in the hand of the Almighty, to whom the praise. . . . Three hundred thousand piasters at the lowest. . . . Ma sh' Allah! It was too much to ask of any man! . . .

" O my dear, O light of my eyes, O my breath! " cried Shems-ud-dìn, when he could speak for amazement. " Why hast thou kept silence? Is it for this thou didst shun me? Fie on thy pride! Thou hast a share in this business, as in all belonging to me. Talk not of begging when thou hast a trade. There is but little now in my hand; but to-morrow or the day after I will pay thee all I can collect. Of the rest we will speak later. Have no fear! All mine is thine; and, by the blessing of Allah, it may be that my patrimony has increased while thine wasted."

Milhem wept on his brother's neck and called him kindest of the sons of Adam.

" By my life, he has earned the right to bear me company," he murmured as he went his way. " May

Allah requite him! And if, in such close converse, he should discover a little thing to my disadvantage, it is so decreed. Allah knows, a man of my employments cannot keep the habits of a saint."

He vowed before God to keep strict watch upon himself, to avoid giving offense to his brother's piety. But he had forgotten the vow, or recanted, when the day of departure came.

Shems-ud-dìn, with other turbaned voyagers, was in the customhouse, patiently enduring the chicanery of a number of small officials whose end was bakshìsh, when Milhem passed down the middle of the great shed, escorted by the mûdìr and a group of high officers. He overlooked Shems-ud-dìn's salutation, appeared unconscious of his neighborhood. In loud talk with his companions he walked out at the farther doors, through which the dance of violet waves shone twinkling, and his brother was left to conclude his bargain with the customhouse men, when a nod from the Sultàn's plenipotentiary might have released him.

On the steamship, bewildered by the novelty of his situation, alarmed by the pushing of rude Franks, Shems-ud-dìn herded for countenance with a little group of the faithful on the fore part of the deck; nor dared to look round for Milhem. The shores and the fair, great city were slipping fast away, ere he descried the latter standing amidships. He ran to him with intent to embrace, but was checked by the formality of his reception.

"Leave me alone here, I entreat thee," said Milhem, as if his teeth were set on edge. "Afterwards, upon land, I will explain all things."

Shems-ud-dìn withdrew, much hurt. He made no further claim on his brother's notice, but sat all day long in the company of three Turkish merchants, men of substance and of imperturbable phlegm, who spoke in proverbs between long sucks at the narghileh. At the rising of the night, when the evening prayer was ended, his black servant brought him food, and spread a bed for him beneath the stars. Once, ere he lay down, his ear caught the voice of Milhem at no great distance talking glibly in a foreign tongue, and by the light of one of the lamps he could distinguish his brother strolling amid a crowd of Franks, both men and women. They kept laughing the senseless, heathen laugh that knows not past or future, nor foresees the judgment of the last day.

The faces of Shems-ud-dìn's companions were lost in night, except when the charcoal in the bowl of a narghileh glowed up redly as its owner drew on it. One said:

"Allah created different animals. He made no crossbreeds. These latter spring from sin. What can be said of one who, being circumcised and duly shaven like ourselves, yet chooses to sit on a chair at a table with infidels, his hands unwashed, to eat abomination, and to toy with unveiled women whose face is of brass for all men, who know not shame? Shall such an one treat us as dirt, being most likely the son of some pimp or other? May the justice of God overtake him, and that suddenly!"

"Now Allah avert that curse, for the man is my mother's son," said Shems-ud-dìn sadly.

"Ma sh' Allah! Is it truth thou speakest? Then Allah forgive me! Let it be as though I had said nothing. I guessed not, O my lord, that he was the son of any honorable house. Most of these officials are the sons of nothing. Why comes he not to sit with thee? May Allah teach him the way of the upright!"

The speaker, a good old man, by name Yûsûf, a dealer in cotton goods, sucked hard at his narghileh. From that hour no one of the sedate circle referred to the great man on board, or betrayed the slightest interest in the doings of the Frankish passengers. Time glided smoothly for Shems-ud-dìn in their company, though few words passed, and those of abstract wisdom. It seemed matter for praise to Allah that there was no chatterer among them. And ever the steamboat panted on over that silken sea, tossing back its mane of dingy smoke along the furrow it had plowed. Only when the panting ceased awhile, did the faithful quit the pose of resignation, uncross their legs, rise, stretch themselves, and praise God for the view of some white town that rimmed the sea, with minarets and distaff cypresses, and fertile gardens on the hill beyond.

At length, near dawn of the fifth day, Shems-ud-dìn awoke to find the ship at rest on the bosom of a wide bay. Already a whiteness played upon the ripples. Already, above high mountains in the east, appeared a blushing streak, a fluttering pulse of light that throbbed and spread till shapes grew clear in silhouette upon the shore line, here a palm tree, there a dwelling; and still the sky to seaward was night blue and spangled with stars.

Shems-ud-dìn knelt down and prayed with fervor, prostrating himself many times. The sun rose, and its rays struck upon his two hands held before his face as he prayed. There were the heights of Lebanon, towers of darkness up against a glory. By the mercy of Allah, he beheld those heights once more. His heart was full.

Later, when the sun rode high and many boats had put forth from the shore, he embarked in one of them with his friends of the voyage, and was rowed to the customhouse. There, engaged in the civilities preliminary to the gift of a coin, he was surprised by Milhem. He leaped at the sound of his brother's voice hailing him with words of love, and the flush of pleasure overcame him. The Bey showed a paper to the officers, who straight made reverence. Shems-ud-dìn and his friends were free to go where they chose.

"I have saved thee and those quaint worthies a mejidi apiece. Art thou not grateful?" laughed Milhem, as they issued forth into the morning sunlight.

Instantly their ears were assailed with the shouts of carriage drivers, and a mob of porters pressed on them, shouting also and gesticulating, shouldering one another roughly in the strife for employment. The Bey had one arm round his brother's neck. With the other he signaled to the most importunate of the carriage drivers, who shook his reins in triumph; the while he continued:

"Praise to Allah, that ordeal is ended. May all the Franks rot painfully, and their fathers be consumed with fire! But it is the will of the Sultàn that we mix with them and learn their ways. For me, to hear is to obey. What am I but a servant? . . . I proceed to the city Esh-Shâm by the coach this evening. That Greek dog, my secretary, follows with the baggage. There I obtain my soldiers from the Wâly—a hundred only, not half enough to overawe those wild beasts. Go thou, upon arrival in that city, to the khan of Ahmed Effendi, the same who was the steward of our father's property. I shall seek thee there. . . . Allah be with thee now and always, O my beloved!"

He kissed Shems-ud-dìn very suddenly on both cheeks, sprang into his carriage, and was driven to a foreign hotel.

His brother, left thunderstruck, stood by the door of the customhouse, impervious to the frantic efforts made by porters, and others having an interest in new arrivals, to attract his notice. He scarcely heard his servant speak to him, and answered at random a question as to whither they should be going.

"So his Excellency the Bey has flown again," said the voice of Yûsûf, the old merchant, close to his ear. "Well, Allah knows where such birds nest! I know not, nor greatly care to know. Wilt thou make the journey to Esh-Shâm with us who are plain men? With Allah's leave we will hire baggage animals, and buy each one of us an ass whereon to ride. We shall journey slowly, by easy stages, being old men and burdened with fat. If thy youth can bear with our infirmities, journey with us and welcome, for we love instruction, and it is seldom that a learned sheykh of the religion falls to our lot for company."

"Let it be as he says, O my lord!" pleaded the negro eagerly; for he tired of standing still, a gazing-stock for low people.

"So be it then," said Shems-ud-dìn, with a cordial smile. "By my beard, I thank thee; for in this minute I knew not where to face."

So it happened that Shems-ud-dìn entered the city of his birth one morning, riding soberly upon an ass, in the company of three fat old men, riding each likewise upon an ass. The legs of all four stuck out wide over full saddlebags. On foot beside Shems-ud-dìn went his faithful negro, now walking, now trotting, in accordance with the donkey's pace. From Zebbadâni, where they had spent the night, they ambled by garden ways to the great city, down a valley full of shade, and the song of birds, and the ever-sweet murmur of running waters.

Shems-ud-dìn had found the journey anything but

tiresome. And now, in the familiar streets where every sight and sound recalled his childhood, he felt like nothing more than a happy child.

Near by the khan of Ahmed Effendi, in a covered way narrow and crowded, where the cavalcade had to go in single file with shouts to clear the path, a hand grasped Shems-ud-dìn's arm, and the voice of Milhem snarled:

"Get down! Get down, madman!"

With fear the traveler alighted, holding his donkey by the bridle. The rope was promptly snatched from his hand and thrust into that of the negro, who stood grinning by.

"Go on—on to the khan! Destroy that beast! —hide him!—drown him. Y' Allah!" hissed the same voice of authority and anger.

More and more alarmed, Shems-ud-dìn faced Milhem. The latter seized his arm.

"Come away! This way or that, what recks it? . . . And now, peradventure, thou wilt deign to inform me why, in the Holy Name, thou masqueradest as a jester, riding upon an ass, preceded by three old men, all on one pattern, all of them also riding upon asses; so that people, deeming it a portent, ask: 'What means this strange riding?' Thou couldst well afford a fine horse apiece for thyself and thy servant. What ails thee that thou must needs play the mountebank?"

"I must return to my friends," said Shems-ud-dìn, disengaging his arm. "They will wonder what has befallen me."

"Thy friends! . . . That absurd procession! . . . Allah witness, it is a child!—a little child!" Milhem raised eyes to heaven, while his laugh rang out. "Must I tell thee that thou art a great man here? All the learned await thy visit with impatience. They would have ridden forth to meet thee. And behold thee seated upon the sorriest scrub of an ass that ever I saw; preceded by three old men, all the sons of one mother, all born at one birth, all as like as camels. What can one say? It is a miracle, perhaps!"

"They are not brothers, neither do they in aught resemble one another," said Shems-ud-dìn, much aggrieved. "They are my good friends. Howbeit, to please thee, I will sell my donkey and buy me a good horse before we ride together."

"That is well. For didst thou come riding upon an ass, attended by three old men with but one face between them, I should know thee for a wizard and depart quickly."

With that Milhem went off, chuckling; leaving

his brother, crestfallen and mystified, to find his own way to the khan of Ahmed Effendi.

Milhem's words proved true. Shems-ud-dìn found himself in high request among the erudite of Damashc-esh-Shâm. During the weeks spent there, he was constantly visiting and being visited; twice was he called upon to preach in the great mosque; and a general meeting of the doctors was convened on purpose to debate with him upon certain knotty questions of religious law. To his vast surprise, Milhem attended him everywhere, lending a disciple's ear to his disquisitions, and treating him in public with a new respect. In private, he condescended to explain:

"O my dear, it is well for one like me to secure the good word of these reverend ones; who, as a rule, hate the government and its servants. I would have them perceive that I am not irreligious in the likeness of other officials. And I thank Allah for thy great holiness, O my brother!"

"Call me not holy!" cried Shems-ud-dìn in horror. "There is none holy save God alone. I give thanks for thy goodness, O light of my eyes! Very kind hast thou been to me these last days. Nevertheless, I shall rejoice when we ride out from hence. It tires me, all this honor undeserved. My head aches with the burden of it."

At length came the morn when Milhem rode forth from that city at the head of a hundred armed horsemen. Certain of the notables of Esh-Shâm bore him company a part of the way, and many of the learned paid the like compliment to Shems-ud-dìn, who cut no mean figure in the cavalcade, mounted as he was upon a coal-black charger, richly caparisoned with housings of gold and scarlet and light blue. Out through the orchards they pranced in the cool of morning, and peasants at work among the trees stood idle a space to admire their bravery. Anon the orchards gave place to vineyards, the vineyards in turn fell away, and the desert rolled out before them, smooth and bare. Then, a halt being called, the promenaders from the city took leave of the serious wayfarers.

" It is the pilgrim's road. You face the kibleh! " one called to Shems-ud-dìn. " Allah hold you in safe keeping! "

Shems-ud-dìn rode beside Milhem at the head of his retinue. Their way led straight across the brown waste—a track a mile wide marked by the horde of pilgrims wending yearly to Mekka. Here and there, upon the sky line, rose a wave of faint blue mountain. The sun shone hot on their left cheeks.

Milhem was in high spirits. Ever and anon he

turned in the saddle to gaze with pride upon his suite, who rode at ease, smoking cigarettes, talking and laughing lightly together.

"Art thou happy?" asked Shems-ud-dìn.

"Very happy. Praise be to Allah who has freed my hand at last. I have not known such elation since the day when the Muscovites fled from before Silistria."

"Silistria! Wast thou really there? I have not heard thee speak of it. The story, I beseech thee."

"I speak but of the joy felt by all believers when the place was relieved. I was not of the heroes."

"But thou thyself hast done brave deeds, O my brother?"

"Yes, surely," said Milhem; and he proceeded to recount a few of them.

That night, in a pavilion pitched on the open plain, the guards lying upon the ground without, around their watch fires, Shems-ud-dìn could not sleep for the wonder of those tales. Himself a timid man, he loved to hear of wild encounters. He strove to place himself in some of the perils braved by Milhem, and thought he would have died of fright.

There seemed no end to Milhem's strange adventures. On the morrow he remembered more of them, which he told with a wealth of homely circumstance which enabled Shems-ud-dìn to witness all he heard. For the listener, those long marches passed as the Thousand and One Nights must have passed for King Shahriar.

They left the plain and entered a land of rocks, where the horses picked their own way gingerly. Here progress was, perforce, much slower. At length, after noon of the fourth day, he reached a height whence, their guide informed them, they could catch sight of their destination. Immediately a dispute arose among the soldiery, some vowing they could see a fine city plainly, while others as positively asserted that there was nothing of the sort within view. Milhem made use of his field glass, a marvel he loved to display, then handed it to his brother. At first Shems-ud-dìn could see nothing; but suddenly he became aware of rocks, and houses like to rocks, of monstrous ruins and a few poor fig trees, the whole presented in a rainbow light not of earth.

"A sweet, a charming place!" said Milhem bitterly.

They descended a rough slope to a ravine, which led on to other ravines; so that more than three hours elapsed ere they again beheld the little town, this time close at hand. A motley crowd of men occupied a hillock at the entering in of the place, above the thrashing floors. At sight of the horsemen this crowd broke in a trice and ran helter-skelter down the hill to meet them. There appeared some strife among the runners, each trying by every means to retard a neighbor. Some were knocked down; some rolled together, struggling among the rocks.

"Allah have mercy! Behold, trouble already! A feud, if I mistake not," said Milhem, as he watched the race. He spoke a word to the chief of the soldiers, who repeated it in a louder tone. The troop pulled up, smartly, on the alert.

Two young men, an Arab and a Circassian, had distanced all competitors. They ran beyond reach of one another, converging upon the spot where the Governor had halted. As they drew near, it seemed the Circassian had a slight advantage, but so slight that they were about to collide, when the Arab caught his rival's trousers to fling him back. The other turned with a yell, felled his adversary, and knelt upon his belly. A knife flashed on high. It would have fallen had not some one caught the arm that flourished it. There was a moment's tussle. The Circassian turned to face his new assailant, when all at once his resistance died away. With a curt laugh he dropped his blade.

"Who are you?" he said to the soldiers, who

now surrounded him. "I would have eaten that dog and all of you into the bargain. Not yours the victory. It belongs to that man there. I looked in his eyes while we fought, and they disarmed me; there was no wrath in them."

"Capital! Most marvelous!" cried Milhem. Forgetting dignity in his excitement, he sprang down off his horse and embraced the hero of the hour. "Thou, the timid one, to perform such a deed! Even I, who am called courageous, had hesitated to come between that wild beast and his prey."

Shems-ud-dìn was near weeping. He could not believe that it was indeed he who had shown such presence of mind. He felt weak now, and dizzy, incapable of any action whatsoever.

By this time the crowd of townsmen had come up. Alarmed by what had happened, they stood silent by until the Bey remounted, when another rush befell, another struggle. "A boon, O our lord!"—"A boon!"—"Hear him!"—"Hear him not!" came the conflicting shouts. There seemed every prospect of a bloody fight under the very nose of the Sultàn's appointed peacemaker.

At a word from Milhem, the soldiers surrounded both factions.

"Where is the sheykh of the place?" shouted the

great man furiously. A tall old man stepped forward, making reverence. " Where the chief of the colonists? "

" I am he! " bawled the prisoner insolently, from between the troopers guarding him. " My name is Hassan Agha, and the title Guardian of the Frontier was conferred upon me by express firmàn."

Milhem smiled. " Release his Excellency at once. Allah forgive the indignity offered to one so great and powerful. By the Koràn, I took thee for a common murderer. Deign to come a little nearer! I would get down off my horse and offer him to your Highness were I less weary with traveling."

The man approached, shamefaced, while a titter spread among the crowd.

" Stand on my right hand, O Great Guardian of the Frontier, and thou, O sheykh, on my left. . . . Praise be to God! " he cried suddenly. " His Grace, Hassan Agha, Guardian of the Frontier, deigns to stand beside my horse. O honor! "

A roar of laughter went up from crowd and soldiery.

" Show a little mercy, O my lord! " whispered Hassan wretchedly. " Am I not shamed enough? "

Milhem did not answer. With the heads of both factions as it were at his saddlebow, he made haste to inform himself of the grounds of dispute between them. On the one hand, he learned how the Circassians would pay for nothing, how they were a turbulent crew, the worst of neighbors, and had even shown disrespect to some women belonging to the old inhabitants; on the other hand, how the Arabs were a set of churls, fathers of avarice, without one generous thought in their black hearts. Shems-ud-dìn, hearing the vigor of those mutual denunciations, judged the case hopeless of settlement without bloodshed. He was amazed to hear Milhem chuckle.

"It is my intention, and the will of the Sultàn is with me in the matter," said the Governor pleasantly, "to live throughout my stay here at the expense of the lord of this place, be he Circassian or the son of an Arab; to reward his loyalty, and that he may boast to his children's children of how he entertained the Viceroy. Now unto the house of which of you two shall I repair?"

The rivals stooped down and exchanged glances under the horse's belly.

"He is the sheykh of the town," said Hassan. "And I have no house of my own."

"He is the Guardian of the Frontier," said the sheykh. "And may it please your Excellency, he has taken my best house and is living in it without rent. A sin it is, and a great loss to me."

"Your honor does not mean to ruin either of us?" coaxed Hassan, glancing up at the great man's face.

"In sh' Allah, he does but jest," muttered the sheykh, with fervor.

"I have the power," said Milhem sternly, "and by Allah Most High, I will quarter myself and all my retinue upon that one of you who first breaks the peace. To-night my camp is pitched beyond the town. You have heard my judgment. Go!"

The old Arab and the young Circassian fell back together, grinning at that clever judgment. But presently the latter returned and clutched Shems-ud-dìn's stirrup.

"As for thee," he cried, "thou shalt lodge nowhere but in my house. I swear it."

"Yes, go with him, O my brother," said Milhem, as one well pleased. "It seems thou art a tamer of wild beasts. Go with him and Allah with thee."

So it happened that Shems-ud-dìn and his servant supped and slept that night in the house of a wild brigand, whose talk reeked of gore. And when he awoke in the morning, there was Hassan watching him from the arched doorway, where he stood polishing a long-barreled gun with a piece of goatskin. They smiled the one to the other.

"Watching thee asleep, I have found out why thou didst overcome me yesterday—me, the pupil of the mighty Shamil; thou, a peaceful doctor of religion. It is because thou art a saint!" said Hassan Agha.

"Allah witness I am the least saintlike of men," said Shems-ud-dìn, yawning to fuller consciousness. But Hassan would have it that he was a saint.

"I go presently to see thy brother," he added after awhile. "We need horses if we are to fight the Bedû. He is a devil, that brother of thine. I expect he will help us with some stratagem. . . . By Allah, it is a thankless task, protecting these tillers of the rock. They have been wont to pay to the chiefs of the desert a tribute, by virtue of which they were unmolested. Now they scowl on us because we forbid all tribute save to the officers of our lord the Padishah—that is, ourselves. As yet we have not seen one Bedawi. The whole nation, they say, is far away in the east at this season. They come not here before the first rain. But these fellahìn are great liars. They told us there was a forest close at hand, but when we looked, behold! a few old terebinths scattered over as many hills. They told me there were tigers, but after hunting the region near and far, I brought back but one lean partridge, some conies, some pigeons, and an owl or so. There are no tigers. Perhaps there are no Bedû either."

Hassan spoke in a jargon approaching Turkish interspersed with words of Arabic. Shems-ud-dìn understood what was said, though he would have been puzzled to separate the words. The friendliness of the speaker was, at all events, past question. He clapped his hands and a girl appeared from some inner chamber, bearing a tray, whereon was bread and curds and fruit, which the negro took from her and set before his master.

"It is my woman," said Hassan casually. "Thou hast not brought one with thee? A pity! Thou wilt sigh in vain. Now there is the daughter of my uncle—he who commands the colonists at Ain Tûbeh, six hours from here—a fine girl, plump and tractable. My uncle would resign her to thee at a fair price—that is, if he have not already struck a bargain with the dealer. It is a custom from of old with us to sell the pretty ones. So they become the mothers of great men, perchance even of the Sultàn's majesty."

"I have not given thought to woman these many

days," said Shems-ud-dìn, with the look of sad remembrance. "My fair one, my Leylah, died in childbed awhile since, my desire with her. A long story, O my friend! It began at Edreyneh, whither I had gone, by invitation of my friend, the learned Mustafa, to preach throughout Ramadan in the mosque of Sultàn Selìm——"

"By thy leave," broke in Hassan, "the morning calls us. At noon or in the evening we can tell our stories. Come forth now, and let me show thee this place of dogs."

No sooner did they leave the house, than men emerged from adjacent dwellings and walked with them till, ere they had traversed half the town, they headed a multitude. Hassan led the way by foul and narrow alleys to the open hill where stood the remains of great buildings, whose smooth pillars and finely wrought capitals contrasted the rudeness of the modern stonework.

"These are the work of the jinn," said a voice from the crowd. "The devils still hold festival here of nights when there is no moon."

Here in the arena of a ruined amphitheater Milhem's tent was pitched. Around it half-dressed soldiers were grooming their horses to the entertainment of a swarm of noisy children. Hassan went forward to the tent; Shems-ud-dìn, in enjoyment of the morning sun, sat down upon a fallen column with his face to the blaze.

The flat mud roofs of the town formed a succession of terrace steps beneath him, descending to a stony wady, beyond which swelled the wilderness of barren rocks. A patch of verdure by the town spring, a few olive trees down in the ravine, a few poor fig trees among the ruins near to where he sat—all else was bronze and purple of the desert hills.

"Even such a land," he mused aloud, "did our lord Muhammed (peace to him) inhabit of old. Amid such solitudes did the angel of God converse with him to the salvation of man and jinni."

The townsfolk had taken seat around him upon the ruins. All eyes were fixed on his face. At those pious words one said: "It is some holy one!" and the whisper ran apace. It startled Shems-ud-dìn, who had forgotten their existence, when the sheykh of the place stood forth and bowed before him, saying:

"Instruct us, O master! We believe; but ignorantly, having but little knowledge of the Way. Teach us now, we entreat thee."

Then Shems-ud-dìn, looking round upon those eager faces, was moved to pity.

"You can recite the Fat'ha and the belief?" he asked.

Instantly the prayer went up as from one throat, and the shout followed:

"God is greatest. There is no God but God; and Muhammed is the Apostle of God."

"You are not in total darkness," said Shems-ud-dìn, with a smile; and he began to tell them of the dealings of God with men from the days of Adam and Nûh and Ibrahim unto the time of Muhammed, and thence downward even to the present day.

In this occupation, Milhem, coming forth from council with the chief of the colonists, found him at length.

"Hail, O tamer of wild beasts!" he laughed. "It is as if they would swallow thee whole, their mouths are so wide open. It is too hot for thee to sit out longer. Come now into my tent—or return to the house of our friend, the Guardian of the Frontier. By Allah, I must thank thee for his friendship. It is a great debt I owe thee, for he could have done me endless mischief."

"By my gun, he is a devil, that brother of thine!" said Hassan, as they sauntered back through the town. "With one blink of his eyes he constructed a plan whereby we may obtain a stud of the best horses at the lowest price ever known. But that is a secret."

Shems-ud-dìn lacked curiosity. He was thinking how to improve the minds of those Muslims, so hungry for instruction.

In the days which followed, he delivered many discourses in the little tumble-down mosque, and up on the open hillside. He came to love the place and its inhabitants, and could not sympathize with Milhem, whose lips dropped curses on the entire country.

Summer broke at length, with thunder, lightning, and a tremendous downpour. Rain fell in sheets for the space of five days. When at last the sky cleared, there was a new cold taste in the air; a torrent thundered in the gorge beneath the town; green plants began to shoot among the rocks. In a little while the hill of ruins became starred all over with blossoms of the crocus and the cyclamen.

Then Hassan was absent all day long, scouring the hills with his men, armed to the teeth. Each evening he spent in cleaning and polishing his beloved weapons.

One night he came in with eyes of joy.

"The Bedû, O beloved! I have seen the Bedû! Their tents blacken a dell not two hours distant. Their herds roam at large. They will come hither for the accustomed tribute. Ah, thy brother is a devil! To-morrow and, it may be, the next day also, I abide in the house with thee. Dost wonder why? Ah, that is a secret!"

Two days later, as Shems-ud-dìn sat meditating beneath a fig tree on the hill of ruins, shrouded horsemen came riding out of the east. His eyes made out twenty of them, each armed with a long lance whose point glanced in the sunlight, each well mounted on a prancing steed. Then, remembering the veiled words of Hassan relative to the tribute, he descended in haste to the town.

Standing at the junction of two narrow ways, he saw the foremost of the cavaliers ride up to the sheykh's door, before which a few children seemed to loiter. The sheykh came forth, crying welcome, and offering his house by a gesture. The leader jumped down and made fast his horse to a stone of the wall. His followers also alighted, tethering their steeds in like manner. They all entered the house with friendly words to its owner.

No sooner were they gone than from every dwelling beside the way, out of every lane, poured soldiers and armed Circassians. The throng prevented Shems-ud-dìn from seeing what happened after. But a fearful din arose; shrieks, curses, laughter mingled with the clash of arms. He stopped his ears. The sky above the hovels turned black in his sight, the houses livid white, a grin beneath frowning brows.

Presently, one came running blindly, moaning as he ran—a man well stricken in years, no other than the sheykh himself. A tall, slim girl ran after him, barefoot and weeping, her veil displaced. Shems-ud-dìn caught the old man's hand and ran with him till the town was left behind. There the frenzied wretch broke from him, and flung himself down in a place of stones, dashing his face upon hard rocks, cursing the day that he was born. Shems-ud-dìn and the girl raised him up between them, and in so doing their eyes met. She bethought her of her veil; in haste she dragged the white lawn across her face, while the little pout of annoyance in self-consciousness became her well. It seemed to Shems-ud-dìn that he had gazed once more in Leylah's eyes—profound as a night of stars when no moon rises.

Despite all attempts to calm him, the sheykh went on shrieking and tearing his raiment. He plucked off his turban and adherent tarbush, and cast them from him, exposing his naked poll to the sun of noon.

"Allah witness, I was forced to it!" he yelled madly. "The sons of Eblìs forced me to betray my good lords. They sat as guests in my house when the soldiers took them. Their horses are stolen, they themselves taken to serve in the army. O Lord! . . . Allah knows the deceit was forced on me. Hassan—may his father perish!—swore to slay my three sons if I refused. We had peace till he came. Now we shall never know peace any more. For our lords of the desert will avenge this outrage. The Circassian pigs will not suffer, for they have no property. But we . . . O Lord! Would to God I were dead and in the tomb!"

Shems-ud-dìn replaced the skullcap and turban upon the old man's head. When the frenzy had somewhat abated, he advised him to seek some neighbor's house; and watched him shuffle off, leaning upon the arm of the tall maid who hid Leylah's eyes beneath her veil, and had not said farewell. Then he himself strode frowning in search of Milhem.

His Excellency sat in the guest chamber of the sheykh's house, flushed with triumph, the Circassians praising God around him. He was in the course of dictating a report of the affair to the Greek, his secretary, when Shems-ud-dìn stood in the midst and cried shame on him. For one minute he seemed startled. The next he turned his eyes toward the vaulted roof, crying:

"Allah witness, it is a child—a little child!"

"Now I know why thou wast loath to have me journey with thee. And I confess here, before all these men, that I did wrong not to be ruled by thee then, that I did wrong in cleaving to thee. For great grief is come upon me. My brother, once the best of men, has sinned most heinously, and I am witness of his crime."

"Said I not he was a saint?" said Hassan triumphantly, from somewhere in the background.

Milhem frowned, stroking his close beard, then smiled indulgently.

"What dost thou know of statecraft? Go, O my brother! and when thou art recovered I will speak with thee," he said, with some compassion and much dignity.

"I go," said Shems-ud-dìn curtly, and stepped forth once more into the sunlight.

That night, as he sat with Hassan in the house, the latter mocked at his grave looks.

"Art still vexed about thy brother's little stratagem? Let not that trouble thee. It is war, thou understandest. The Bedû will take vengeance for this, and we, in turn, shall avenge their vengeance, and so it will go on—in sh' Allah—till the last day."

"My thought is not of war," said Shems-ud-dìn.

"Know, O Hassan, that I love once more!" And he related his adventure with the old sheykh's daughter. "O her eyes! O her straight white nose! O the fullness of her cheeks, her chin! . . . Now tell me, what character does she bear?"

"Thou wouldst not wed her, surely?"

"I love—that is enough. My life flows out to her. There is but one beloved!"

"Ma sh' Allah!" murmured Hassan, in the utmost consternation. "She is a girl like another. There is nothing told of her. A virgin has no form, no color, no fire, save that one gives to her. For me she is nothing; for thee, much. As for character, she has none, which means she is a young girl. . . . But reflect, O my dear! When thou returnest to Istanbûl——"

"I shall not return."

"Ma sh' Allah!" muttered Hassan again, and he kept silence a great while, munching his long mustache. At length he said, "I must inform thy brother, my lord the Bey, of this thy decision."

"Tell him," said Shems-ud-dìn.

On the morrow he was roused betimes by Hassan's hand on his shoulder.

"Arise, O my soul, and come with me to my lord the Bey. I have seen him already."

It was a gray dawn threatening rain. In silence they repaired to the house which Milhem had occupied since the approach of winter. The great man sat upon his bed to receive them.

"O Shems-ud-dìn, what is this?" he cried reproachfully. "Is it true thou wilt abide in this wilderness worse than Jehennûm? Surely thou art mad. There, at Istanbûl, thou art in the road to great honor. By Allah, I look to see thee Sheykh-ul-Islâm. Whereas here—what awaits thee? . . . And canst thou contemplate a lasting union with the daughter of a base fellâh—thou who couldst make a grand alliance to enhance thy honor and mine? I beseech thee, think not of it! If thou doest this through disgust of what befell here yesterday, know that those men are rebels against the Sultàn. They owe more than the worth of their horses to the government. And how light their punishment! They are but asked to serve three years in the army, like every faithful subject of his Majesty. By Allah, there is no wrong done to them! . . . Say, was that the reason of thy mad resolve? . . . The term of my appointment draws nigh, and it makes me sad to think of leaving thee here in this lair of wild beasts."

"I am content to be here," said Shems-ud-dìn

firmly. "Once have I sinned in forsaking the path God showed me. I will not sin that sin a second time."

"But Allah pity! What can a man of thy wealth and attainments do in a place like this? It is not a place one could beautify for a wonder and a byword. I myself have had that dream: to change a desert to a paradise. But what can a man like thee do here?"

"He can live in peace; he can teach the people; he can ply his trade in the bazaar. As for my wealth, I have no need for all of it. When thou regainest Istanbûl, sell all I possess, and take the half of the proceeds to thyself, sending me the other half. I shall give thee letters to my steward and also to the heads of the learned. Thy need is greater than mine."

"Allah, look! It is a child—a foolish child!" cried Milhem loudly; but he was somewhat moved from opposition to his brother's scheme. "Thou talkest of peace. Remember yesterday. That is nothing—a trifle—a mere beginning. . . . Peace forsooth! Nay, my soul fears grave danger for thee."

"Fear not, O my lord!" said Hassan, who had all this while stood silent by. "On my head be the danger. This, my good lord, thy brother, is not one who can guard himself. He is not like thee, a devil! Thou hast said it: he is a child—a little child, whose hand is in the hand of Allah. The friendship of such an one is counted to a man for righteousness. By Allah, I am glad he stays with us. His presence calls a blessing on us all. But would to Allah he had chosen the daughter of my uncle. It would not have been half so serious. As it is, we must swear peace with those fellahìn forever and ever."

"Said I not well when I named thee tamer of wild beasts?" said Milhem laughing. "But I would thou hadst chosen some pleasanter way in which to display thy power. I ask but one thing of thee, thou dear madman. Let me depart ere thy wedding. I would not defer thy bliss, but fix it for the day of my departure; so thou shalt not mourn my loss too deeply. I shall start at the dawn, leaving my peace with thee. By Allah, it is a disgrace to our house. Nevertheless, do as thou wilt. It is thy business."

The day whereon Milhem's government expired, Shems-ud-dìn rose two hours before daylight, mounted the horse which Hassan had saddled for him, and rode slowly to his brother's residence. The town was astir. Lights moved here and there as yellow eyes in the darkness, illuming spaces of rough wall and filthy pathway. He had to shout his way through the crowd which choked the approaches to the house of the Bey.

The cavalcade stood ready to start, bits jangled, stallions neighed. The soldiers standing at their horses' heads, in hooded ulsters and high, long-tasseled fezzes, cut a queer figure as seen in silhouette against the shine of sundry lanterns borne by members of the crowd.

At the noise of his brother's arrival, Milhem came out, when the crowd gave forth a strange, deep note, like a night bird's cry, repeated at regular intervals; and with the note each man beat his staff with might upon the ground. The staves fell as one. The effect was both weird and mournful, by the light of a few scattered lanterns, in that cold hour and in the darkness under the stars.

Milhem was warmly wrapped. He embraced his brother silently, and then in a husky voice gave the word to advance.

The same wild sounds of respect and woe accompanied them to the hill without the town, to ring in their ears long after.

Shems-ud-dìn rode beside his brother through dark chasms of the hills till the white of dawn appeared above the rock ridge toothed like a saw. Then he reined in his horse.

"In thy grace I depart," he murmured.

"With my peace thou goest!" said Milhem, and he gulped as if to swallow something which impeded speech. "Allah knows I sin in suffering thee to remain here alone. My heart reproves mere sorely. Kindest of the kind hast thou been to me always. Often have I been ungrateful; very often have I sinned against thee. I ask thy forgiveness humbly now. Allah knows my soul hurts me! . . . O beloved! . . . Give me now a blessing ere we part."

Milhem sprang down off his horse, and would have knelt to Shems-ud-dìn had not the latter, dismounting also, prevented him, saying:

"Thus only do I bless thee, O my dear!" He kissed Milhem warmly on both cheeks.

For a moment they clung together, white dawn on their faces. Then Shems-ud-dìn whispered:

"God bless thee, O my brother, now, and in the hour of death, and in the last day."

He climbed back into the saddle and rode lonely away, followed by shouts of good will from all the escort. He felt nothing, saw nothing, thought of nothing, for a long while.

Just as he reached that turn of the wady whence

the town is first seen, the sun glanced out behind him. Himself in deep shadow, he beheld all the opposite slope, dwarf town, giant ruins, a few poor fruit trees, bathed of a sudden in a rich glow, like nothing earthly, beneath a sky grape blue and full of stars. He drew rein, gaping at the vision. There were the peasants going to their tillage among the rocks; there were the veiled ones tripping down to the spring, each with arms upcurved to sustain the pitcher upon her head. In that ruddy glow they flitted as thin shades. He could realize nothing, remember nothing. The place seemed foreign to him.

But presently a horseman galloped forth from the town, and rode straight toward him, clattering upon the rocks. Shems-ud-dìn heard his shout. It was the voice of Hassan, crying:

" Hail to the bridegroom! "

Then Shems-ud-dìn blushed hot for joy. Even now the bride prepared herself. It was his wedding morn.

CHAPTER I

MANY years had passed since that day-spring. Shems-ud-dìn sat in his shop in the small bazaar, a great sorrow at his heart. His wife had died long ago; his son, lured by promises from the exalted Milhem, had gone forth to try his fortune in the government service; and now it had pleased God to smite the last remaining of his dear ones.

Alia, little Alia, whom he cherished as his own eyes, lay sick of a wasting illness none could name. Every homely charm and nostrum had been applied in vain. A famous leech from distant Damashc-esh-Shâm had bled her copiously, and stayed ten days in the house, expecting some good result. At last, seeing her life still waned, he had taken Shems-ud-dìn aside and spoken gravely.

" O Sheykh, this is from the hand of Allah. All my science is as air against it. The stalk is cut, the ear will fall. It is decreed. Grieve not overmuch, I entreat thee. Rather thank Allah that it is not thy son, but only a girl from whom no honor comes."

Shems-ud-dìn duly thanked Allah, but cast about

in his mind for some remedy yet to try. He was come to his shop at this idle hour of noon on purpose to think undisturbed. But the halls of his understanding were darkened and unfamiliar; even the lamp of faith burned dimly, a great way off. Though he prayed, "In mercy heal her! O Allah, spare the sunshine of my age!" he knew the worthlessness of such prayer. His will was not lost in the Divine Will, but beat against it to its own hurt, a moth at the flame.

The voice of the torrent in the wady, swollen from days of rain, droned in his ears. The noontide murmur of the town—men's talk, the cooing of doves, a clink from the forge—was subdued by it. It filled all the pauses of thought with a dull refrain which seemed that of his own woe, the ever-recurring numbness of sheer grief that prevented his thinking to any purpose. It deadened a noise of bells approaching, until it was quite near, in the bazaar itself.

The clangor filled the air suddenly, starting many echoes. But Shems-ud-dìn did not turn his head. He continued sitting with his back to the world, spreading out his hands over the brazier, which he had lighted for an illusion of comfort. He heard the ponderous, padded tread of camels; he smelt their hides; and one by one, in passing, the huge beasts took the daylight from him. The jangle of the bells was deafening.

All at once it ceased. The train had halted. But Shems-ud-dìn did not turn his head.

"O Allah, weld my will to Thine! O Lord, spare my daughter!" he kept moaning.

"For how much dost thou sell this, O effendi?" said a husky voice behind him.

Turning then, in some dismay, Shems-ud-dìn beheld a man unkempt and meanly clad, grinning sheepishly as he held up a tiny bottle of attar of roses. It was evidently one of the camel drivers, for he held the end of a rope wound round his wrist; and the small, superb face of a camel looked over his head into the shop, sneering at what it saw there.

"For how much?" came again in the husky voice. "I give thee six piasters."

"Be it thine at that price. Take it, my son, and go in peace."

The grin departed from the camel driver's face. His mouth fell open, and his eyes grew round with alarm. He set down the bottle hastily, and began muttering to himself.

"What ails thee? Why dost thou murmur in thy soul?" asked Shems-ud-dìn.

"Ma sh' Allah! Thou askest why? Is there

not cause enough, O my master? Is this precious attar—the soul of a thousand roses? By Allah, no, I think not. For six piasters! And if I bought it and carried it to her I love, and a jinni came out and deflowered her I love, and slew me and took my love away under the sea or among the roots of the mountains. . . . Aha, precious attar indeed! and cheap at six piasters! . . . But Ibrahìm is a wary man, one accustomed to look behind him. When he saw thy back toward him, when thou gavest him no greeting, he said in his soul, 'O soul, be warned! Either this merchant will play the listless to drive the harder bargain, or else here is something strange, out of the natural——' "

" Be silent, foolish one!" interrupted Shems-ud-dìn. " My daughter, in whom I delight, lies near to death, and my mind is distraught with grief. Though I heard thee and saw, it conveyed nothing to my mind. In truth, the perfume is worth more than six piasters. Take it as a gift from me and go."

At that the simpleton kissed the ground before Shems-ud-dìn.

" O father of mercy!" he blubbered. " Long have I desired to make such a present to her I love. Allah comfort thee, O my dear lord! Despair not for thy girl. There be workers of miracles in the land nowadays. Hear what befell myself awhile since. As I journeyed to the Holy City in the train of certain Franks, having charge of their baggage, death seized me round my belly and flung me from my mule whereon I sat, and laid me upon the stones of the path, and there knelt on me with such weight that I shrieked aloud for the pain in my midst. It had been the end of me, had not one of the infidels, who was a physician, jumped down off his horse, and producing something from his clothes, forced me to swallow a part of it. Its taste was bitter as gall, so that I screamed the more and cursed the poisoner. But after a little, death fled and my health returned to me, and I went forward singing upon my way. Great is the science of the Franks. Our physicians are as fools to them. They have a fine hospital in El Cûds. Take thy daughter thither. . . ."

"Ya I-bra-hìm!" came a cry out of the distance. "Where art thou? Make haste! We tire of waiting."

"The companions call me. In thy grace, I go. Forget not my counsel. What is the journey to El Cûds for one like thee? Three days, or four at the most; and the girl can ride comfortably in a palanquin between two mules. There, with Allah's leave, she will be healed. . . . I come! I come!"

Tucking the bottle into his waistband, he turned and would have run, had not the camel, refusing to be hurried, pulled him up with a jerk. The rope between them was taut as a lute string as they passed from sight.

The jangle of bells had sunk once more beneath the roar of the torrent ere Shems-ud-dìn perceived that his prayer was answered. Then great awe fell upon him, and he said in his heart, " I have sinned." It shamed him to know that Allah had heard his wayward moaning. He, an old man whose beard was white, had prayed blindly, senselessly, as a child prays, to be shown a little hope, some remedy yet untried. Now that his request was granted, he felt as that camel driver had felt on finding the attar his at the price first offered.

While he sat thus between great hope and fear, a face looked in upon him out of the sunlight, and a youthful voice exclaimed:

" May thy day be happy, O my master. How fares the beloved? "

It was Shibli, his favorite pupil and the bridegroom designate of Alia.

" Enter, O my son, and welcome," said Shems-ud-dìn; and he straight described to his disciple all the happenings since sunrise, from the departure of the city physician to the advice so strangely proffered by a simple camel driver. At the end, Shibli cried:

"It is the best advice. Let us go to El Cûds. Apart from the virtue of a pilgrimage to the Dome of the Rock, I thirst to behold so famous a city. My father will grant me leave to travel with thee. O happy day!"

Shems-ud-dìn smiled upon the boy's excitement. To rebuke it, he said:

"Allah knows it is not for pastime that I go."

But Shibli's delight in the prospect made it bright for him also.

Presently, giving his disciple charge of the shop, Shems-ud-dìn issued forth into the sunlight and started to climb a steep and stony path, like the bed of a torrent, which led to his dwelling. Women, gossiping at their doors, blessed him by name as he passed, and inquired tenderly concerning the health of his dear one. The sun, sinking down upon the hilltop, dazzled his eyes. Hope, renewed, opened the gates of his mind, even as his despondency had shut them fast, to things around him. He noticed the lizard basking in the sunshine, the tuft of hyssop growing between the stones.

His house stood highest of all in the little city, close upon the hill of ruins. He had himself planned and superintended its building long ago, so that there was none like it for size and nobility of aspect.

Before the wide open arch which was the entrance hall, upon a terrace of rolled mud—which seemed a parade ground, but was in fact but the roof of the house below—an old negro was standing in a posture of some dejection, gazing wistfully at the heights beyond the wady. He started at his master's approach, and answered the question about Alia with a despairing grin.

Shems-ud-dìn passed into the house. Very softly he opened a door. The room within was darkened. What light stole in through chinks in the shutters revealed but vague outlines.

"How is she?" he whispered.

"As always. She has not slept." Some one arose in the gloom and came to him.

"Who is it?" wailed a fretful voice from the floor. "O Fatmeh, who is it? Bid him depart."

Shems-ud-dìn went and knelt beside the sufferer. "See, O beloved! I have brought thee a thing thou lovest well—some of thy chosen perfume!"

"I love it not. I hate it! I hate everything! O Allah, kill me quickly! . . . I would sleep. O Fatmeh, take my father away that I may sleep."

Fatmeh followed the sheykh to the door, and clutched his robe.

"Hear me, O my lord!" she whispered. "She is not better; she cannot sleep. What can one do? I will tell thee. Be not wroth with thy servant. There is a tree not far from here—a good tree and efficacious, for all thy frowns—one that has healed thousands. Let me tear off a strip from her finest garment and go myself and hang it on the tree. So, in sh' Allah, she will be healed and no one know the manner of her healing. Cast me not off. Hear only, I entreat thee. Let us make but trial of the tree. How can it be a bad tree? Did not Allah make it with the others?"

"Be silent!" said Shems-ud-dìn sternly. "Allah forbid that one of my house should commit so great an impiety!" With which he passed out from her and shut the door.

By that time the evening shadow covered town and hillside; only the summit of the minaret shone like the henna-dyed tip of a finger pointed heavenward. But the cliffs across the wady still basked in broad sunlight. The figure of the old negro, lounging in the archway, stood out darkly on that distant glow.

Shems-ud-dìn sat down in the entrance and remained in profound meditation, his every thought a prayer; while the flower of sunset bloomed and faded upon the cliffs beyond the wady, and blue night stole upon the landscape. Then, out in the gloaming, a cry arose—a long-sustained yell, breaking anon into a wild unearthly chant. It came from the minaret, which the piety of Shems-ud-dìn himself had added to the little mosque. Its burden of memories brought tears to the old man's eyes.

He arose and went out on to the roof of his house. A star sparkled on the fading green of sunset. A cool breath from the hills fanned his cheeks. Falling on his face toward the kibleh, he prayed Allah to abate something of his too great love for Alia, which had broken the calm of resignation becoming his age, which hung as a cloud between him and the Creator.

When he regained the porch, old Mâs was hanging up a lantern to a hook on the wall.

"O Mâs, go to the house of the excellent Hassan Agha; if he be within, beg him to honor me with his presence here."

"No need," grinned the black. "Even now I hear his honor's voice without."

In confirmation, there came a shout, "Peace on this house!" and the Guardian of the Frontier appeared in the entrance arch. Behind him a crowd of heads, but dimly seen, were bowed reverently. Hassan's men—a fierce-eyed, swaggering crew—followed him about always like tame dogs. With a shrug and his grin, Mâs went off to pound coffee for the invaders.

"What is this I hear of thee, O my eyes? Thou goest to El Cûds under advice of an angel from Allah? Shibli told me the strange story as I rode through the bazaar at sunset," said Hassan, after salutations. "Hopest thou still for the girl? By my gun, it grieves me to see thee seek the cause of misfortune, going groping like a blind man, when the cause is plain to all besides thee. Thou hast let the girl grow between thee and the Praiseworthy; wherefore the Almighty slays her, as one breaks the small branch of a tree, that He may see thee. What do I with my mare if one praises her too warmly, so that my pride in her leaps up to flout the Most High? I say piously: she is thine. I give her in haste to him who extols her. I put the occasion of sin from me. And so I would do with my daughter did I sin through her."

"The right is with thee, O Hassan," said Shems-ud-dìn, in great distress. "But—O my pearl of pearls! O my Alia! O young moon rising on my night of years! Darkness were my portion without thee! My woman is dead, and I have not the heart to enjoy another. My son is far away, and his love grows cold. I have received no answer from him these many months. But my Alia—she is here, my soul itself. Allah forgive me, I must try to keep her."

"I say naught against that, O my eyes, but only against the extravagance of thy love for her. Obey the angel certainly. The Franks have skill in medicine—more especially that tribe of them which is called the English. One Englishman, who was in Kars during the siege, healed my father's brother, and a thousand others who were counted dead of the Yellow Wind. The power to cure is their inheritance from Isa the Prophet, the mighty healer. Proceed to El Cûds. Thou art like to behold thy son there, by what I heard to-day from the mouth of a camel driver from that city who had much to tell of one Abd-ur-Rahman Bey, an officer in the garrison, and nephew to the glorious Milhem Pasha. It can mean no other than our friend, thy son. He came thither from Istanbûl three months ago."

"Three months!" ejaculated Shems-ud-dìn, with downcast eyes.

"Yes, certainly thou must journey to El Cûds, if

only that the sight of him may refresh thy soul. But tell me, O my dear, what is the right of this story of an angel? Shibli said only that an angel had appeared to thee, and bidden thee take him (Shibli) to El Cûds, for the sake of Alia, somehow."

"Not so," said Shems-ud-dìn. "The truth is quite otherwise. Indeed, it is more likely that he who appeared to me was a devil." Therewith he told the plain story, the Circassians listening with open mouths.

"Ma sh' Allah! A jinni, very surely," said Hassan, at the end. "I myself observed something peculiar in his aspect. Not often is so long a train of camels sent forth without money in the hands of the drivers. Yet—believe it, who can!—on three men, having charge of more than fifty camels, we found but half a bishlik, two poor knives, one brass button, and a bottle—a very small bottle—of attar of roses. No doubt, but the man was an afrit, who spoke with thee. Devils love to attack a saint, just as I would rather kill a big, strong Bedawi than a little weak one, when it comes to avenging their slaughter of my two sons. Yet fear not, O my soul! A man of thy works can laugh at all the jân. I myself will journey with thee, and, while the Frank physician heals thy daughter, I, with Allah's help, will procure new rifles for my comrades, a great supply being lately come to the garrison there."

Hassan paused to think awhile, stroking his heavy white mustache.

"Yes; a devil, very certainly; perhaps even Eblìs in person—Allah knows! The thing is proved. You have heard, all of you here, how a devil cannot profit by the gift of a holy one; how the gift will presently return from him? Well, behold this small bottle of attar of roses!"

He held up the phial so that all could see. A shudder of applause ran round the circle.

CHAPTER II

Two hours before daybreak, Mâs, the negro, stood on the hill of ruins with a donkey saddled and bridled. One of his hands grasped the tail of the ass for insurance against braying; the other held a lantern, its rays diverted from the house of Shems-ud-dìn. Mâs looked up at the stars with a dissatisfied grunt. He observed in his soul:

"Now Allah correct all women! She whispers, 'At the seventh hour be ready for Alia's sake,' and I leave my couch and the comfort God sends to me in dreams—the rich banquet and the palace of gurgling fountains, the sweet brides, and my youth restored—I forsake all that, because of her whispering, and I saddle the ass and take light in my hand, and stand out here in the chill——"

A noise of cautious and uncertain footsteps here broke his reflections. He stood intent to listen. All at once came the rattle of stones displaced, a thud, a smothered scream. Promptly he turned the lantern so as to throw light on the disaster.

A woman, closely veiled and muffled, rose slowly up from off a heap of refuse.

"Is it thou, O Mâs? Praise to Allah! Say, what was it smote me that I fell?"

"Come," said Mâs simply.

Fatmeh tottered forward and clutched tight hold of the negro.

"O Mâs, I dare go no farther. Take thou this piece of raiment—the raiment of the beloved—and go and hang it on the blessed tree."

"Alone?" Mâs laughed to scorn the notion. "I love the dear one, but go alone by night to a chosen haunt of devils, I will not! In the daytime ask me."

"Allah forbid! Is it not a secret for the dark to hide that thou sayest 'in the daytime'? 'The daytime!' Allah, listen!"

"Since our lord gave thee leave to go, what is to hide?"

"Leave! Allah knows he has given leave enough. A sin, indeed, if recourse might be had to Frankish wizards and not to that gentle tree!"

"Then come. We waste time."

Seeing she would still have tarried, scolding, Mâs lifted her up and placed her bodily upon the donkey's back. Then taking the headrope in his hand, he strode forward.

No sooner did Fatmeh recover breath than she

began to inveigh against all male creatures, but principally those on whom the wrath of God is manifest in a black hide. Things, she declared, were come to a pretty pass when a slave dared order the goings of his mistress, and carry her whither she would not. But to all her tirades Mâs replied tranquilly:

" Since when art thou my lady? Thou art not all thou wouldst be."

After a time words failed her. Only a moan, when some exceptional roughness made her bump the pack saddle, assured Mâs that she was still there behind him. At length she besought him, whimpering:

" O Mâs, speak to me; I am afraid. Tell me, O kind Mâs, a story to beguile the way."

" I know no story."

" Sing then. For the love of Allah, sing a little."

" I will not; for the jân love music. When the day comes, then perhaps I will sing."

Fatmeh appealed to Allah against such hardness of heart. She looked up at the stars for comfort. But the folds of her veil obscured the view of them, and when she looked down again the darkness seemed alive. Save the clap of her donkey's hoofs, there was no sound audible upon those unseen hills. The ray from the lantern danced on ahead like an evil spirit. All at once, to her horror, the dark earth yawned before her, spinning dizzily to a shape, like clay upon the potter's wheel. In a trice there was a vast black bowl, in whose depths glowed fire, small specks that grew and joined, dwindled, and grew again till all else vanished. She lurched forward, groping for Mâs; but in the gloom her hands missed him, and she fell to the ground.

When she came to herself again, she was dazzled by the light of the lantern shining full in her eyes. Mâs bent over her, his black face burnished in the light.

"Y' Allah! What ails thee? Come, arise, I say."

She moaned: "Woe on us! The fires! The fires of punishment!"

"Ah!" smiled Mâs, as seeing light at last. "There is a camp down there in that wady—whether of the Bedû or the gypsies, Allah knows. Now come, since thou art not dead."

Again he lifted her on to the broad saddle. Again an impenetrable darkness closed about them. But she was no more afraid. Having passed the extreme of horror, whole by a miracle, all else that might befall seemed light to bear.

A whiteness crept up somewhere behind the night. Soon, with the vagueness and the ceaseless jogging, she fell asleep, and awoke to find herself in a plain, somewhat cup-shaped, rimmed with jagged rocks. Something gaunt and monstrous, which appeared writhing, yet was still, stood in the way against them. It was the tree.

With a thankful heart she slid down from off the bruising saddle. She took from her bosom the strip of Alia's raiment and gave it to Mâs, who was tall and could reach the branches.

" It is finished," he said presently, with satisfaction.

Light increased with every minute. Mâs, having put out the lantern, withdrew from her and went and knelt upon the ground, his left shoulder toward the dawn. But Fatmeh, sitting huddled beneath the magic tree, knew not, nor cared to know, what he was doing. She wept in repentance of her great audacity.

She was aroused by a sound unexpected and terrible—the gallop of many steeds. The noise drew near apace. A voice cried:

" Halt at the tree and rest."

At that she flung herself face downward upon the ground and knew no more, until a conversation arose so close to her that it was matter for wonder how the speakers escaped contact with her body.

"It is a Bedawi, I say."

"It is some beast."

"Pronounce, O Nesìb the Thief, thou lord of two good eyes. What seest thou?"

"I see nothing marvelous. Yonder is a man in white raiment, praying toward Mekka. And here, not far distant, is a black donkey at grass, bearing a pack saddle, but no load thereon."

"Ha, ha! Is there light to tell black from white?"

"Others may not, but the Thief can surely."

"The man is a Bedawi. Let us take his head with the others. So shall my sons be avenged. Praise be to Allah! We know now that they go to El Cûds, these dogs; and we go also to El Cûds. Are they not between our two hands? . . . Yon wretch has finished his prayers. Let us slay him and reap his head. . . . What kind of man is he? I cannot see for the light beyond."

Fatmeh could bear it no longer. She screamed aloud in her alarm for Mâs. Immediately she was seized and lifted, struggling, to her feet. Men thronged upon her. She smelt men and horses.

They had pulled aside her veil, yet knew not who she was; not one of them had seen her face before. Her knees gave way, her tongue clove to the roof of her mouth. She could only moan and whimper under indignities, and think with terror of the Sheykh Shems-ud-dìn. For disobedience this shame was come upon her.

"Stop! Hold your hands! . . . O my lord Hassan, I beseech thee, let her go. She is of the house of my master, the Sheykh Shems-ud-dìn," cried the voice of a man out of breath—the voice of Mâs.

On the instant, as it seemed to her, she was free. She straightened her veil, clutching for support at the saddle of the horse nearest to her. But instead of the saddle her touch encountered the bristled skin of a head—a man's head. She gave one look ere her shriek went forth. There were two of them, with bloated tongues protruding.

At her cries a laugh went up from the horsemen.

"Wilt ride with me?" asked Hassan Agha. "It falls not often to the lot of woman to roll two men's heads at once upon her knees. Have no fear, my daughter. They shall not bite thee. . . . Nesib and thou, Ali, stay and guard these people. Be mindful to use them with respect for the sake of the saintly Shems-ud-dìn, to whose house they belong. Allah be with you."

He had risen in the act to spur his horse, when

Fatmeh, repressing her terror of the ghastly heads, caught his stirrup.

"O my lord!" she entreated, "of thy goodness breathe no word to the sheykh, my master. He knows naught of my coming hither——"

Hassan cut short her prayer with a loud laugh.

"Then say nothing to thy lord of my two heads. Call it a bargain, O my dear!"

And he rode off at speed with his men in the sun's first rays.

CHAPTER III

WHEN Shems-ud-dìn set forth from the town, there was great excitement. Babes were held up by their parents to watch the saint ride by. A cry arose that he should bless the place; and he did so, sitting on his old white horse, adorned with old trappings of scarlet and light blue and gold which had not seen service for twenty years. The little city on its hillside, then, in the early sunlight, looked restful as a flock of sheep at noon. There were tears in the sheykh's eyes as he turned and rode away.

He rode alone, with eyes downcast, his beard upon his breast, never far from the palanquin which contained Alia and her nurse. Shibli, in the pride of youth, galloped ahead with the Circassians, the sunshine glancing from their accouterments as they darted in and out of the shadows flung by great rocks across their path.

The poles of the women's litter were borne by two mules, one in front and one behind. Beside the hinder trudged Mâs, armed with a long goad. He crooned as he walked a sad song without end, some echo of his long-lost childhood in hot Darfûr. Now and then a groan came from within the litter, and Fatmeh was heard soothing her charge. Once the curtains parted, and Alia looked forth smiling at her father.

"How is thy health?" he asked earnestly.

"The better for being free of that dark chamber, that hateful town, always the same smells, the same thoughts. Now, in the sun and sweet air, I am well, O my father!"

"In sh' Allah!" murmured Shems-ud-dìn, and he bowed his head.

But as the heat increased, and shadows shrank away, nothing but moans came from within the palanquin. The Circassians, tired of display, came back one by one. Shibli, ranging his steed alongside that of Shems-ud-dìn, prattled incessantly without regard for his listener. The sheykh heard the talk around him as a buzzing of flies.

"What gift bearest thou to the Frank physician, O Nesìb?" cried one of the riders to his comrade near at hand.

"A fine one, O my eyes! I bear an old-time garment, the best of my inheritance. It belonged to my father's father, and has been as an heirloom in the family."

"Capital! Allah will give to thee. . . . For my part, I take a trifle, a mere nothing. The chief's command was on every man to bring some present in his hand. And I had nothing, being a young one, newly married. But I remembered to have seen clouds of bees upon a certain rock in the wady below our house. So I went, bearing fire with me, and slew those bees and took their honey, a portion of which is here in my saddlebags. My woman wrapped it for me and put it in a jar. In sh' Allah, the infidel will accept of it."

"In sh' Allah, but it is no great thing," returned he of the garment.

They proceeded by the easiest and clearest road, which was also by much the longest, so that for the sake of the litter they spent four hours upon a distance which the horsemen alone could have covered in less than two.

At length they reached a little plain, or cup-shaped hollow, among the hills, in the midst of which stood an ancient terebinth full three parts dead. A number of rags hanging from the withered branches gave to that tree a curious bearded look.

"We will halt awhile in its shade," said Hassan, who had assumed the chief command. "The sun is hot; and after a little, Allah sends to us the midday breeze, when it will be more pleasant riding."

At that Shibli, with a shout, set off galloping toward the tree. At his shout a flight of small birds forsook its branches and flew, wavering, with faint tweets, toward the northern hillside. With a scream of delight, the youth unslung the gun from his back, leveled it, and fired after the birds. In a second his horse was standing on its hind legs, and he himself lay on his back among the stones. His gun had flown a great way off, in another direction.

A roar of laughter went up from the cavalcade. The women peeped forth, tittering, between the curtains of the palanquin. Only Shems-ud-dìn betrayed concern.

"Art hurt, O my son?" he inquired, dismounting amid a general stampede in chase of Shibli's horse, which was by that time careering madly across the plain, showing the flat of its hind hoofs to the pursuit.

"This is a lesson," said Hassan Agha, chuckling. "Boys must learn from Allah! Did not I warn thee to have a care in handling thy gun? Did not I tell thee how to sit for firing—bridle dropped, feet forward, pressing the stirrups? Yet when the time came, thy feet were somewhere behind thee and thou didst drag up the bridle. Another time, perhaps, thou wilt remember."

Shibli arose, crestfallen, tears trickling down his cheeks. He admitted with shame that he was unhurt.

The litter was set down in the shade. The beasts were hobbled and turned loose. The men who had gone in pursuit of the runaway returned successful, their horses panting and half-blind with sweat. All crowded together beneath the tree.

Shems-ud-dìn sat with his back to the trunk, where the shade was darkest. It was nowhere a continuous blot of shade, but rather like a net enmeshing forms and faces. Nesìb the Thief, who had brought a waterskin along with him, gave to drink in a horn cup, to the sheykh first, and then to all the company; not forgetting the women, upon whose needs Màs waited.

By and by, as they sat in drowsy converse, came a sighing of the branches overhead. Flowers that grew among the stones swayed a little. It was as though a cool hand fell on every brow. The breeze which tempers noon had found them out.

Throughout the halt Shems-ud-dìn gazed straight before him, or else upon the ground at his feet. Not until Hassan gave the word to remount did he raise his eyes in thanksgiving for that half-hour's refreshment. They remained fixed in awful contemplation.

From the lowest branch of the tree, just overhead, hung a strip of brightness, fluttering, among other similar strips by no means bright. This strip was new, the rest were very old. Moreover, a sunbeam threading the maze of twigs had singled it out for illumination. The sheykh stared and stared. Those colors—green and white in stripes, with a slender thread of crimson down the green—were most familiar. He had bought a piece of silk of that pattern not long ago of a traveling merchant, and had made of it a garment for Alia.

He turned toward the litter. A hush had fallen on the group around him.

"O Fatmeh, come forth! Whence is this silken rag? How comes it to hang here?"

"Rag! What rag?" screamed the woman, creeping out through the curtains. "Allah witness! What have I to do with it? Is it my tree that I should be held accountable for all that grows on it? Allah forbid! . . ."

Her voice, which had arisen shrill and brazen, soon quavered and broke. The grins of the Circassians cut the ground from under her. She fell on her face before Shems-ud-dìn, in a paroxysm of repentance.

" How often have I forbidden thee all traffic with this tree? A wrong to myself I had forgiven; but this is an insult to the providence of God. Henceforth I wash my two hands of thee. Return to thy kindred, and may Allah bless thee! "

Fatmeh rolled on the ground in convulsions of shame and grief. She shrieked to the bystanders to slay her then and there. But the sheykh stood by his horse, obdurate. He surveyed her contortions without mercy, till a new voice of lamentation smote his ear.

" O Lord! . . . O my father! . . . Be not so wicked! . . . O Allah, turn my father's heart to pity! Wouldst thou slay me quite, now, immediately? Thou knowest I am nothing without Fatmeh! I will die—yes, die now—and punish thy wickedness. Oh, woe upon us! Woe! Woe! "

The thin face of Alia looked forth unveiled between the curtains. It was distorted with pain and fury, most ugly to look upon. Shibli made a wry face behind her father's back. It was the first time for many months that he had seen the likeness of his betrothed.

The sheykh stood gaping, at a loss for a word.

" Arise, O woman, and resume thy place beside her," he said at last lamely.

The spectators smiled and shrugged shoulders one at another. But in a moment their looks changed to horror.

The Sheykh Shems-ud-dìn lifted his right arm and, taking hold of the bright rag, pulled with might. The silk tore with the shriek of a living thing. He threw it away and straight remounted his horse, heedless of the piercing cries of Fatmeh.

CHAPTER IV

THE first night of travel was spent at a village occupied by a colony of Circassians. Here, naturally, they met with a warm welcome. The guest chamber of the head man was allotted to Hassan and Shems-ud-dìn; Alia and Fatmeh were accommodated in the same house; and the rest of the party found hospitable quarters, though the most part slept, from choice, under the open sky.

Shems-ud-dìn retired early, craving leave to mount to the housetop and drink the fresh air of night. For long he paced the terrace roof in the darkness, then sat crosslegged awhile, then, as his limbs felt cramp, arose and walked again.

The great heart of the night beat loud in his ears, and he fancied he could hear respirations, as its cool breath fanned his cheeks.

By and by the eastern hill grew black and imminent; a coronal of light appeared; and the moon pushed up her horn, a golden spearpoint against the stars. The flat-roofed houses took shape suddenly, cube by cube. A minute since they had been lost in night's mystery, at one with the dim hills, the starry sky.

Shems-ud-dìn's prayer ceased not. He prayed for strength in submission. An instant fear haunted him, making this night most terrible. He thought that God would take the life of Alia at once, without delay, and so ratify the covenant of the tree. In tearing down the idolatrous rag from off the branch, he had accepted his daughter's death at the hand of the Lord. He prayed for perfect resignation. But a wish would outrun the prayer—oh, that Allah would appoint some other victim, as He did of old for Ibrahìm, His friend!

With the first dawn he went down into the house to wash before the morning prayer. When his host inquired if he had spent a happy night, he answered Yes, and thanked him kindly. Alia yet lived; nay, Fatmeh pronounced her better than on their arrival the evening before. So the sunrise smiled to him.

That day their road led through a forest of terebinths, not dense, but growing singly, or else by clumps of two and three. The path was pied with shade, affording a pleasant diversity; and Alia often looked out from the palanquin with cheerful words to her father.

It was late afternoon when they came forth from among the trees. From a bald crown they surveyed a waste of yellow hills tossed and crumpled in the likeness of a stormy sea. They halted, without dismounting, to inhale the keen air of those highlands.

Of a sudden Hassan laughed out, and pointed to the valley right below them. In the midst of a green-stained dell swelled a brown mound, in shape nearly oval. By one end of the mound moved a camel, by the other a man.

" He must have been to sleep," laughed Hassan, " and have let go the rope. And now if he catch it ere the Day of Judgment, it will surprise me."

When the man stole round to one side of the hillock, his camel, which till then had been browsing peacefully, lifted its head and stepped round to the other. They could see the headrope dangling as it ran.

The man stood still, in thought apparently; for soon, as if struck by a new idea, he started to climb the mound. From the top he caught sight of the camel beneath him, placidly chewing. They could hear his yell of triumph as he rushed down upon it. But he pitched headlong—and by the time he reached level ground his camel was not there.

The man sat nursing himself.

"Now he weeps, I assure you," cried Hassan, exultant.

"Let us go down and help the poor man," said Shems-ud-dìn.

"No, that we will not! It were a sin! But I am with thee, my dear, to go down and hear his tale. It must be a rare one. Ma sh' Allah!"

Already Shibli and the younger men were urging their horses down the steep decline. Old Hassan followed at a breakneck pace. Only Shems-ud-dìn and Mâs the negro stayed by the litter. Care for the sick girl obliging them to descend very slowly, step by step, by the time they reached the foot the rest of the party had been some time gathered round the lord of that froward camel. Shems-ud-dìn drew near the group.

The fellâh was about finishing his tale of woe. He moaned:

"O Lord, I possess but this one only, and a person in Es-Salt, the lord of much wealth, would buy him of me for a journey he makes to-morrow. The price offered is a high one. I would fain receive it. But to-morrow will be too late; the merchant will have gone his way. Would to Allah I had not lain down to sleep! Would that I had never been born to need sleep upon the earth! Be kind now, I entreat you, O my masters! Help me to recover my camel."

But the Circassians, and Shibli with them, mocked his anguish, saying:

"We sympathize with thee; that is understood. But we be plain men. We meddle not with signs and wonders. Who ever saw the like of this thy quandary? Surely it is upon thee from the hand of Allah."

At that the poor man put his knuckles to his eyes and wept aloud, cursing the stock of men so heartless.

Shems-ud-dìn frowned upon their wickedness. He was about to use his authority on the man's behalf when lo! the camel itself came striding round a shoulder of the hill and stood within a few paces of him. The rest beheld not the chance, intent on their evil game.

Very quietly the sheykh walked his horse toward the great beast, which watched his approach without concern, nor demurred even when he grasped the headrope.

"O fellâh, behold thy camel!"

For a moment all were petrified. Then wild cries arose: "A wonder!"—"A sign from Allah!"—"The Lord has ordained a miracle at the hand of the saintly Shems-ud-dìn!"—"Run, O poor man!

Make haste to kiss the earth between his horse's feet!"

The fellâh did as they bade him. He ran, and falling on the ground, flattened himself before the horse of Shems-ud-dìn, crying:

"Deign to ride over me, O favored of Allah! Behold, I am the dust of thy pathway!"

The sheykh made him rise, and explained to him the occurrence as most natural. "Seeing thou hadst ceased from pursuing, thy camel tired of playing alone and came of his own accord to look for thee."

But the owner of the camel would not be convinced, any more than would the bystanders, that the event was less than a miracle. The Circassians congratulated one another, whispering:

"Now is it clear that he knows the language of beasts; for how else could he read the mind of this camel, that he is tired of playing alone? By Allah, he is no less than a prophet. Praise to the Highest, who has made us his companions."

"Where sleep you to-night?" asked the camel's master, wiping his eyes on the sleeve of his robe.

They answered him: "At Es-Salt, whither thou also goest."

"Good. Then I travel with you."

Throughout the rest of the journey, which was very monotonous, the eyes of that fellâh dwelt upon Shems-ud-dìn, raptly staring as at a vision. In the town of Es-Salt it would have been hard to find a lodging for the women, since the only khan was filled with a caravan bound to Bûsra from the Holy City; but this man took them to the house of a friend of his, who, on hearing the case explained, turned out with his family into the adjoining stable, and so made room for them. And when Shems-ud-dìn arose in the morning and looked forth, there was this same man squatting patiently beside the threshold.

At sight of the sheykh, he fell down and kissed his feet.

" May thy day be happy, O my master! I seek a boon of thee. Grant me but leave to journey with thee to the Holy Place. I will be no charge upon thee; for I have this hour received the price of my camel."

" But thy business!—thy house!—thy woman!"

" Those are always with me. They await my return. But as for thee, thou passest. It is an occasion to be seized."

" But—Merciful Allah!—I travel not for pastime, O my son."

" I know, O my lord. Thy companions have

already told me; and I sorrow with thee. How is the health of the lady, thy daughter, this morning?"

"In sh' Allah, it is no worse. She yet lives," said Shems-ud-dìn sadly.

"May Allah heal her quickly! Deign now to give me the saddlebags. I will make ready the horse for thy Grace."

He would not be gainsaid.

CHAPTER V

WHEN the cavalcade assembled without the town, this new companion came riding upon the sorriest ass ever seen, which, it transpired, he had borrowed from a friend. He took all the laughter at his expense in excellent part.

His name, he said, was Zeyd the son of Abbâs. He had been born in El Arìsh, toward the country of Masr, but had not beheld that place for many years. Bred to the calling of a muleteer, he had led a wandering life from childhood. It was now three years since he had settled down in a certain village, about six hours distant from the spot where they had found him at hide and seek with his camel. He had taken to wife a girl of that place, and was fairly prosperous as poor men reckon.

Not half of all he said reached Shems-ud-dìn's ears, which were strained toward the palanquin; but a word of courteous acquiescence contented Zeyd.

They came to the end of the highlands in a bare brown shoulder thrust out over a chasm wide and deep, no mere wady of the hills like those they had hitherto traversed, but a trench cut below the surface of the world. It parted the mountain lands to east and west. Upon the plain in its depths, through mists of heat, they could see the belt of foliage coiling like a snake, which marked the course of the river. In the south, at no great distance, the valley widened to inclose a dazzling sheet the eye avoided, a memorial of God's wrath, the Sea of Lot.

Here they came up with the Circassians and Shibli, who had stopped for consultation.

"What sayest thou, O my dear?" cried Hassan. "Shall we rest to-night in the plain yonder; or, for the day is yet young, shall we push on nearer to El Cûds? Decide, I pray thee."

"Let us hasten onward," replied Shems-ud-dìn.

His prayer all yesterday and this morning had been that Alia might die in a house peacefully, that death might deal gently with her, as would not be the case did she expire amid the jolt and rocking of that crazy palanquin. He was therefore for pushing on as far as might be.

But soon after they began to descend, the path being steep and rough so that the mules moved jerkily with frequent slips, a shriek came from Fatmeh within the litter; and when all halted and crowded round, Alia was discovered lifeless.

Mâs, with the ready help of Zeyd ebn Abbâs, lifted her out and bore her, duly veiled, to where a jutting rock spread a fan of shadow. Everyone thought her dead.

But Fatmeh, with a snort of contempt, bade them all stand back. She removed the veil from the girl's face, and began to chafe one of her hands, bidding Shems-ud-dìn do the like with the other; she wetted her fingers in her mouth and laid them to Alia's forehead; with the result that presently the life returned. Alia drew a gasping breath and her eyelids fluttered.

"Praise to Allah!" cried the onlookers.

"Praise to Allah, in truth!" cried Fatmeh, with a point of scorn. "Small praise to anyone else here present! It is the fatigue, of course, O my poor one, O my dove! How should it be otherwise when she has been jarred so many hours in yonder box, which would kill even a jinni, I think, with its lurch and the creak of the poles. Let her lie in peace to-day, and she may live to see El Cûds. Hurry on, and she will die on the way! Allah knows that, for truth."

There could be no further question as to where they should halt for the night. Alia was carried back to the litter, and they resumed their march down into El Ghûr.

They reached the plain a little before noon, and dismounted near a village of seeming ant hills at the foot of a thicket, on this side the ford. Here food was procured for the sick girl—curds and fruit, and rice boiled with the daintiest parts of a fowl—of which she took but a mouthful ere resigning the dish to Fatmeh. But she drank deep from a pitcher of cold pure water, and lay back, seeming refreshed. The women abode in the litter set down in the shade of some trees, the hovels of the village appearing to Shems-ud-dìn far too wretched to receive them.

The repast ended, Hassan and the rest crossed the river and strolled off in various directions. Only Shems-ud-dìn and Zeyd ebn Abbâs stayed with Mâs beside the litter. The last named busied himself in constructing a rough booth with boughs and reeds and grass, and garments borrowed from one and another. Shems-ud-dìn sat in a state between prayer and meditation, observed with reverence by his new disciple. The soothing voice of Fatmeh, the voice of a nursing mother lulling her babe to sleep, blent with the coo of doves among the trees. A knot of villagers watched from a distance, impressed by the stillness of the strange men.

At length, when shades grew long to eastward,

and Mâs, having finished his work, had gone to bathe in the river, Zeyd ventured to say:

" Deign to teach me somewhat, O my master."

" In the name of Allah, gladly," consented Shems-ud-dìn, starting to consciousness.

Taking suggestion from the scene around them, he told of Lût and Ibrahìm the Friend, and how Allah destroyed the wicked cities which once stood where now the bitter sea shone gold to the setting sun. The villagers—men, women, and little children—approached to listen, edging nearer shyly, like wild things fascinated, till they formed a half-circle before the narrator. Soft breathed " Ma sh' Allah! " punctuated his discourse. The Circassians, returning by twos and threes, lounged upon the ground within earshot. " It is a great saint, hear him! None like him in all the world! " they whispered to the breathless fellahìn; till Shems-ud-dìn observed how they whispered among themselves, and ceased speaking, in some annoyance. Till then he had been scarce aware of their presence. It was no time for preaching, his sorrow told him, nor for aught else wherein his soul took pride.

The villagers stole up, one by one, to kiss his hand, and he suffered it, but begged them to withdraw; which they presently did, with many a backward look. Certain of the women returned at nightfall, bringing slabs of bread, and earthen bowls full of curds and cooked meats, which they set upon the ground near him. They stayed not to haggle over the price, but took what was offered them and went away.

"Ma sh' Allah!" said Hassan Agha, with his thunderous laugh. "It is good to travel with a holy one. To-morrow, it is likely, we shall find coined gold instead of stones in our path. Know also, O light of my eyes, that our enemies are delivered into our hands, an easy prey. The Lord knows we must thank thy sanctity for it, under Allah. Some dwellers in the House of Hair camp ahead of us within that crease of the mountain to be seen from here. My own eyes have beheld them. And one, a pilgrim to Neby Mûsa, who stood near, told me all there is to know concerning them.

"They are infidels, coming of a southern tribe which of old was perverted from the Faith; and they go now to keep the feast of the Nazarenes, which is nothing but a battle between two rival factions of that sect, decided annually in the church, called the Resurrection, in El Cûds. This fight is all their observance; for the rest, they have no religion more than other wild beasts. It is good to exterminate such men. In sh' Allah, we shall slay every one of them or ever they behold the city. So shall my sons be avenged!"

"Be not so wicked in thy thoughts," said Shems-ud-dîn sternly. "What are these men to thee? These slew not thy sons!"

Hassan shrugged up his shoulders, and began to roll a cigarette.

"Am I Allah, to tell one sparrow from his brother?"

"Thou wouldst not shed innocent blood!"

"Is their blood innocent? Allah knows: let Him decide. I know that men like to these in appearance slew my two sons ten years ago. . . ."

Shems-ud-dîn arose quivering. "Now Allah reckon with thee at the Last Day! Fight while we travel together, and I leave thee without a blessing! Allah witness, it is my last word!"

"Well," growled Hassan after a long pause, "let there be truce for a day or two till we arrive in El Cûds. There, if they push against us in those narrow streets, I cannot swear to restrain the hands of my followers. But till then, peace. Thy blessing is dearer than the blood of dogs, beloved!"

"Good," said Shems-ud-dîn; and, wrapped in his white cloak, he lay down to sleep upon the ground before the bower which Mâs had built, where slept the women.

So it befell, on the morrow, that a troop of horsemen overtaken upon the mountain road went unmolested. The men had swarthy faces, dark eyes of a smoldering fire, and they spoke pure Arabic with a husky voice. There was a little friendly rivalry, racing of horses and the like, between them and the Circassians; but that was all.

"What doest thou?" inquired Shems-ud-dìn of Zeyd ebn Abbâs, who rode with his eyes shut, muttering.

"I pray to Allah," was the reply; and a little later, when they had parted from the tribesmen: "I praise Allah," he said.

"Thou doest well, O my son."

At a lonely khan, where the midday halt was made, they found a company of Frankish travelers, taking food from off a white cloth spread upon a flat rock. It was a desert place. Blond crags towered up wan against the rich blue; the world seemed of two plain colors—earth and sky. The Franks made a great clatter with knives and forks upon plates of tin or some other metal. They laughed loud and vacantly, rousing echoes among the cliffs. They stared rudely at the newcomers, the palanquin in particular attracting their curiosity. They pointed with knife and fork at the object of their attention; and one who stood by, having the countenance of an Arab but the voice of a Frank, gave them information in their own jargon.

When the foreigners had done eating, they clambered up among the rocks and began to throw down small stones, laughing consumedly for no reason. Their guide was left alone upon the level space before the little khan. Hassan approached him and entered into conversation.

"Surely the Franks are possessed with devils," said Shibli to the sheykh excitedly. "See, they laugh at nothing, they throw stones at nothing, yet rejoice in their vanity. They reject the means which Allah has provided, and eat with strange implements hard to manipulate, making of their necessity a game of skill. And their raiment. Saw a man ever such clothes? The women, more especially; if, indeed, they be women! Look now, I beseech thee, O my master."

"Wherefore look, O my son?" said Shems-ud-dìn listlessly. Whereupon Zeyd, the son of Abbâs, groaned like a camel, supposing those women to be sinful beyond the common.

Anon Hassan returned from the dragoman, bearing a face of news. He threw himself on the ground, as one heart-weary, ere observing:

"The Holy City is full to overflowing, according to that dog. Allah help all of us to find a lodging. The Nazarenes fill every nook, and a cake of bread is sold for a week's wages. In sh' Allah, it is not all true, what the hog has told me."

"Allah help us, in truth!" cried Shems-ud-dìn. "We shall arrive too late to seek at once the Frank physician. And the city is set on a hill—the air of it is keen. My child will surely die. Allah teach us how to proceed."

"I will tell thee, O my master, and you also, O companions of my lord," exclaimed Zeyd ebn Abbâs suddenly, with a joyful face. "The brother of my wife's sister's husband's father dwells not far from the Holy Place, on this side, at a village of the hills. He is not a rich man, but deign to stay the night with him, and not he only, but the whole of my wife's family will be honored."

Shems-ud-dìn took the speaker's hand affectionately, saying:

"Daily do I praise Allah for the loving kindness of the poor. Surely God has sent thee, O Zeyd of the open heart. The Lord increase thy wealth and hold thee ever in His keeping."

He rose then, and went to tell the women of Zeyd's offer and his conclusion to accept it. A cry of " Praise to Allah ! " escaped from both occupants of the litter. After the glimpse they had just obtained of Frankish manners, neither Alia herself nor Fatmeh was in haste to behold the Frank physician.

CHAPTER VI

THE hills were as negro heads about a fire; twilight, olive-tinted and something luminous, flooded every crevice of the land, as Shems-ud-dìn sat before the house of Zeyd's wife's relation, beneath a tree which grew there, concluding a letter to his son Abd-ur-Rahman. The quality of the light obliged him to hold his face close to the reed as it ran. All who dwelt in that place, squatting round upon the stones, watched him with awe and wonderment.

"After inquiry concerning thy dear health"—so ran the screed—"I set forth to thee that, thy sister the little Alia, having been ill a long while, and all which medical science both local and illustrious could do having proved vain, it occurred to me, by the permission of Allah, and seemed no sin, that I should bring her, thy sister aforesaid, to the city El Cûds, where, according to one who spoke with me of this matter, there are found foreign physicians of a science transcending that of the physicians of our own nation; whither therefore I bring her, having journeyed thus far by the grace of Allah, and intending to abide here this night in the village below mentioned in the house of a friend of one of my companions, a good, kind man, may Allah bless him.

"And moreover I inform thee that all is so far well with me, by the mercy of Allah, thy sister yet alive, though weak and worn to the shadow of her thou bearest in mind; but that hearing of the city that it is full to overflowing of Nazarenes thronging to their feast of the Resurrection, I think well to send thee beforehand this word of our coming, that thou mayest seek out a place where I and my companions of the road, to the number of twenty men, may lodge while we remain in the city; a long time or a short, as Allah wills it; and to express my eager hope that thou wilt meet us in the gate to-morrow early, to inform us where the Frank physician dwells.

"Know further that Hassan, our old friend, is with me, and many also of his people, and Shibli, my pupil and thine ancient playfellow, who all for compassion bear me company; that these all salute thee with every blessing, and that I, thy father, yearn exceedingly to embrace thee once again, and may Allah preserve thee ever!"

This letter, a marvel of fine penmanship, though written upon his lap in the failing light, he delivered to one of the Circassians standing ready beside his horse. The villagers, who had squatted silent throughout the writing, crowded now around the recipient, craving leave but to glance at the superscription. "Ma sh' Allah!" they exclaimed, when it was shown to them. The messenger, proud of his sudden consequence, proceeded to read aloud for their delectation:

"'To the most illustrious, the most glorious, the most renowned, the most honored Excellency Abd-ur-Rahman Bey, the most respectable, may Allah preserve him ever!' So it is written, O my uncles!"

And those simple ones heard with rapture, heads bowed as at a blessing.

Then the messenger sprang into the saddle, and, under guidance of a barelegged youth, rode off with a clatter up the stony path between the houses, out by olive groves to the open hill whose brow cut sharp upon the last of sunset.

When the messenger returned, it was the third hour of night. Shems-ud-dìn sat in the guest room of the village, observed and questioned untiringly by the group of elders. A throng of women, children, and the younger men pressed to the open door, craning their necks to peer within. All those bearded faces lighted from below by a saucer lamp upon the floor in their midst, backed by gigantic shadows, seemed to tower upward indefinitely. The messenger bowed low on entering, his hand on his breast.

Shems-ud-dìn bent forward eagerly. "The answer, O my son! Give me the answer. I praise Allah for thy safe return."

"There is no answer, O my lord," replied the messenger wearily. "On arrival in the city I rode at once to the tower where the soldiers lodge. There I made inquiry of one who stood guard, and he said, 'O my uncle, his Excellency the Bey was within here a while since, but whether he be still here or be gone to his own place, enter thou and discover, for I cannot certify thee.' So I gave my horse to the boy, my companion, to hold—a good boy and a useful; his father is blest in him—and entered in at the gate, questioning all I met. At last came one who assured me that the Bey was gone to his dwelling in the city, and described the house to me and named the quarter and street in which it stood. So I went back again to my horse and repeated the description of the house and its whereabouts to the boy, my companion, who led me by night ways full of snarling dogs, till we came to the house.

"From within came sounds of feasting with song and the voice of the lute. I knocked upon the gate till there looked forth an old man, to whom I showed the letter and its superscription. He went from me, and came again and told me, saying:

"'His Honor the Bey makes merry with his friends. He will not be disturbed. Deign to confide the letter to me, and I will give it to him in the morning when he will hear my voice.'

"So, seeing that the man was old and of a kind countenance, I thought good to give him the letter.

"Then, as I came out from the city, the boy leading me—for alone I had been as a blind bird in a net—two soldiers at the gate would have stopped me, asking my business, and for what cause I rode forth armed. But the boy slipped past them, and cried to me, and when they turned to see who cried without, I put spurs to my horse and galloped by, upsetting one of them.

"The tale is finished, O my master."

"Good; I thank thee," said Shems-ud-dìn, with dignity. But his soul kept murmuring, "No answer! He sent no answer!" And its voice was as the sea for sadness.

Hassan, to cheer him, cried: "Be not downcast, O light of my eyes! Thy son is young, and the way of youth to discretion winds through feasting and carelessness. To-morrow, when he reads thy letter with a clear mind, he will hasten with joy to meet thee. Remember the days that are gone, when thou also wast light of heart."

And all they that sat with them in the room joined with Hassan, saying:

"Thy worthy friend speaks truth. The ways of youth are not as our ways. The wisdom of youth is a bird with no nest. Take comfort, O sheykh! Be assured there is nothing wrong."

But Shems-ud-dìn derived no comfort from their sagacity.

CHAPTER VII

NEXT morning, before the start, Shems-ud-dìn offered money to the lord of the house; but the old fellâh thrust back his hand.

"Is the honor nothing in thy sight? Give a little to my neighbors on account of thy companions, and my peace with thee."

Shouts of good will went after the departing guests. Shems-ud-dìn's heart was lighter than on the night before. He neared his journey's end; Alia seemed no worse; and the shortcomings of Abd-ur-Rahman appeared excusable by daylight.

Suddenly, from a hilltop, they beheld the city. Contained in shadowy walls, its roofs clean burnished by the morning sun, it was a sight to catch the breath. The Dome of the Rock, three parts shadowed, bloomed aloof in its noble precinct. Here and there amid the throng of buildings, some little polished surface caught the light and flashed, a diamond. The whole seemed the masterpiece of some worker in silver or ivory, rather than an old city built at divers times by men unknown to one another.

Of tacit accord the cavalcade had halted to admire, when a hubbub arose among the Circassians. Two dead fowls had been discovered beneath the cloak of Nesìb—fowls stolen from the village they had just left. Loud were the cries of shame. Hassan struck the thief on the head with the butt of his carbine, stunning the wretch, who would have fallen had not a loving comrade sustained him. He took the birds and gave them to one more trustworthy, with orders to return to the village and pay the price of them.

"Oh, the sin! Oh, the shame of it!" groaned Shems-ud-dìn.

But Hassan, chancing to overhear, objected, saying:

"Be not too sad, O my soul! Nesìb is a thief even as thou art a saint. It is Allah's will upon him. He has stolen slippers from the gate of a mosque. And he has his uses. Not for nothing do I admit an Arab in my troop. There are but two of them now among us, Nesìb and one Ali, the friend of Nesìb. Nesìb would not join without Ali, and Nesìb is so useful that we accepted Ali, who serves no purpose on earth, but only hangs upon Nesìb. Ah, our Thief is clever! He would steal the food out of your mouth, and your belly none the wiser."

Shems-ud-dìn smiled at the description; and their talk continued in a pleasant strain till, having crossed a dry torrent bed in the wady, they began to ascend.

They had lost sight of the city all save the walls, which ran along the top of the rocks above them. Shems-ud-dìn's face fell sad once more, as he mused upon the mystery of fate, and the uncertainty of what awaited him up there within.

Lepers and other beggars, seated beside the broad, made road, howled to them for alms. Men with donkeys and mules and camels passed up and down before them. The toll of a mighty bell echoed among the stony hills—the bell of the Resurrection, explained Zeyd ebn Abbâs, calling the Nazarenes to prayer. Everything announced their approach to a great city such as few of them had seen in all their lives. Shibli's excitement knew no bounds. He kept galloping on in front and returning to tell what he had seen, asking answerless questions, laughing and shouting like one possessed.

"Stop! Stop, I say! Are you deaf, all of you? What do you, wearing arms, so great a company? Show your teskerehs before I let you pass."

A soldier stood out before them in the gate of the city, while two more issued yawning from the guard-house.

Shems-ud-dìn proffered his teskereh, but the sentry scouted it.

"That allows you to travel; good. By what authority do you travel armed like soldiers?"

"Look hither. Canst read?" said Hassan loftily; and he held out a copy of that old firmàn naming him Guardian of the Frontier, which he was in the habit of carrying about to confute the skeptical.

"What is this?"

"Canst thou not see? It bears the Tûghra, the handmark of Power."

"Is it some antique?"

"Dog! Dost scoff at the hand of the Padishah? Let pass, or thy punishment shall be horrible. Know that we have with us a greater man than thou ever sawest in all thy life of sin——"

"Is it this man?" broke in the soldier impudently, pointing with his finger at Zeyd, the son of Abbâs, who, on his miserable donkey, in his ragged clothing, cut the sorriest figure imaginable.

"Pig!" snarled Hassan. "I will ride thee down!"

"Have the kindness only, and thy punishment is sure. Once in there, thou and thy friends are caught in a box."

"Deign but to listen. Knowest thou one Abd-ur-Rahman Bey, a yezbashi of the garrison?"

"Of course. What is that to thee?"

"I will tell thee. This holy sheykh beside me is his father. Now let pass."

"Gently, gently, O my uncle. That is good, what thou sayest—excellent—I ask no better. Only —I do not believe it. He of whom thou speakest is a great one. Everything is known about him; yet I never heard that he owned a father living, much less do I look to see his father riding up from nowhere in the midst of a crew of rascals without proper teskerehs— Ma sh' Allah!"

The final exclamation was uttered in a frightened whisper. The speaker stood back hastily with his comrades, sprang to attention, and presented arms.

The road described a right angle under the gateway, so that no one standing without could see through into the street. The guard had stood for some seconds rigid, nosing their rifles, ere he whom they thus honored could be seen of Shems-ud-dìn. Even then, in the young officer advancing toward him, one white-gloved hand on his sword hilt, not running nor manifesting the slightest emotion, he was slow to recognize his only son.

Abd-ur-Rahman came to his father's stirrup and kissed his hand with the same formality which had marked his approach. He murmured:

" Welcome, and twice welcome, O my father."

At sound of his voice a cry went up from within the litter close at hand; but Abd-ur-Rahman seemed not to hear it.

" Thou didst receive my letter," said Shems-ud-dìn, as they passed in beneath the massive gateway.

Abd-ur-Rahman, still at his stirrup, answered:

" In this hour I received it. It should have been delivered to me last night, but for the obtuseness of the doorkeeper at the house where I dwell. As to thy question concerning Frank physicians, I know nothing of the matter. I inquired on my way hither, and have learnt that there exists a hospital kept by one of them. Thou wilt find its direction written on this paper, as also that of a khan where thou mayst find room enough. What was told thee regarding the present fullness of the city concerns not the Muslim quarter. I hope that my sister will be soon healed, and that thou wilt be blest in thy stay here. Now, with permission, I must leave thee. I will seek thee after noon at the khan."

" Allah be with you now and always, O my son."

As he watched Abd-ur-Rahman stride off down a side street of many arches, Shems-ud-dìn wondered what it was that so oppressed his soul.

CHAPTER VIII

BENEATH an arched doorway opening on a tunneled way where lurked so deep a shadow that, on emerging thence, the fall of sunlight hurt men's eyes, sat a fat old man, greasy and no little dirty, making his frugal breakfast of bread and olives. Behind him, through the doorway, basked a little court in sunlight.

His was the quietest, coolest seat in all El Cûds, he was used to boast. Great, therefore, was his consternation when, suddenly deafened with the clatter of many hoofs, he saw his tunnel invaded by a file of armed horsemen so numerous that, peeping forth, he could not see the end of them. At first, being an infidel, he supposed them sent by government to raid the hospital and slay every sufferer. But a further glance convinced him that no such mercy was contemplated. He perceived a close litter borne between two mules. The contrivance had entered the tunnel; it remained to be seen if it would ever get out again. One called:

"Hi, O old man! Is this the Frankish hospital?"

"It is a hospital, that is sure. And it is Frankish in the sense that it is maintained by certain Franks having more money than wits."

"There is with us a maiden, very ill. We have come from far that she may be healed by the Frank physician. Her nurse is with her in the litter. Let them in, we beseech thee, to the presence of thy lord. We bring gifts, and the father of the girl, that sheykh behind there, is very rich. It will be worth much to thy lord if he can heal her."

"Are you Jews?"

"Allah forbid!"

"Is the sufferer of that race?"

"Allah forbid! Why askest thou? Why lookest thou so strangely? Art thou, perchance, thyself of the dregs of mankind?"

"What matter for me? I am but the doorkeeper. But all those who pass within to be healed or die, as Allah wills, must be Jews and Jews only. It is the law of the English to whom this house belongs."

"Ma sh' Allah! Knowest thou, O old man, that this hospital of thine is a place unclean, a place of sin, no better than a lair of filthy swine?"

"I know nothing. I am the doorkeeper. They pay me monthly wages, and my task is light. I say they are good people. They can do what they please, for me. . . . It is plain you are from the country, or you would not be surprised and angry at such little things."

And he smiled the superior smile of the townsman.

"The physician! Ask concerning the physician. I would speak to him without delay," called Shems-ud-dìn, pushing his way on foot to the front.

"He will tell you the same which I tell you—only Jews enter here. . . . But as for a physician—ah, I assure you—he is a physician—none like him under heaven! By Allah, one touch of him cures any disease less malignant than death itself! Go to his house, I advise you; it is not far from here. It is likely he will show mercy to you, for he is a kind young man. Come, I will teach you the way thither. I am the doorkeeper, and cannot quit my post. But perhaps I can find one to guide your honors. . . . O black man, thou canst never turn those mules in the alley there. Lead through into the court where there is room enough. There they can turn at ease, and the poor, sick lady—may Allah heal her—shall not be inconvenienced. Take care now! Oäh! Heed this little step."

In a trice the old doorkeeper had become all politeness, espying a silver coin in the hand of Shems-ud-dìn.

A few minutes later the procession stopped once more before a door, that looked lonely in a place of high blind walls. By that time it was accompanied by a crowd of bare-limbed urchins, beggars, and other idle ones. Zeyd, the son of Abbâs, as riding upon an ass in the midst of horsemen, and conspicuous for the wretchedness of his apparel, excited particular admiration in these adherents. When he got down off his steed and went to help Mâs unharness the mules from the litter, they thronged about the despondent animal, touched and examined it closely, as it had been of gold.

"Do you covet him, O sons of two walls?" called Hassan, with his mighty laugh. "His beauty is for sale, but the price is a high one. Be careful not to steal him."

Whereat a grin illumined those dirty faces, and rows of white teeth gleamed forth. One of the Circassians hammered loud upon the door till an old negro looked out in dismay upon their multitude.

" Is the physician within? Here is a girl near to death. We have come from afar, bringing gifts, that the Frank may heal her."

" Certainly, he is within. Wait a little while, till I inform him of your desire."

The negro shut the door, but reopened it presently announcing his master's pleasure to receive them.

" But not all of you," was subjoined with a grin. " It is a house, not a city. Let those concerned enter, while the rest abide by the beasts."

" O happy day! " shouted Hassan. " An English physician is the best of physicians. One in Kars preserved the life of thousands. Importune him, pursue him, flatter him; give him no peace till he hear thee; so shall the girl have life instead of death."

Zeyd, the son of Abbâs, Mâs, and two of the Circassians bore in the litter, taking each a pole. Through a dim corridor with closed doors on either hand they passed to an open yard, where, by direction of the black doorkeeper, they set down their burden in the sunshine. The pavement of this yard, like the walls and floor of the entrance passage, was so scrupulously clean as to seem of white marble, striking awe into the visitors. Shems-ud-dìn kept close by the palanquin. A third Circassian followed, both arms laden with the sheaf of gifts. Hassan, misliking the looks of the town-bred rabble, stayed without beside the horses, to keep order; and Shibli, for reasons of his own, stayed with him, though invited by Shems-ud-dìn to enter.

The litter deposited in the courtyard of the house, the three Circassians proceeded, with the help of Zeyd ebn Abbâs, to spread out the presents upon the flags so as to be seen to advantage. They were in this occupation when a Frank emerged from a room above them and came slowly down a flight of steps into the court. He was young and of a smiling countenance, very red, after the manner of his kind when sunburnt. His eyes were screwed up against the strong light.

A shout of praise greeted his appearance. All heads were bowed. Shems-ud-dìn ran to the foot of the stone flight with design to kiss his hand. But the Frank resisted. He repaid their salutations fluently, and, for the rest, spoke in a childish kind of Arabic, easy to comprehend. He asked to know in what manner he could serve them.

Zeyd ebn Abbâs and the three Circassians raised hands and eyes toward the great blue sky, implying that the gravity of the matter passed human explanation, and required Allah fitly to describe. Mâs, whose custom was to mind his own business, employed himself tranquilly in smoothing down the curtains of the palanquin. Shems-ud-dìn bowed low before the stranger.

"Know, O renowned hakìm, that my daughter, who is here with us, lies sick unto death. And it was told me in the place where I dwell, how thou canst heal where all others despair of healing. Wherefore I journeyed hither under escort of these kind companions, bringing the girl my daughter, and certain gifts for thy acceptance, and also a sum of money, that peradventure thou mightst take pity on my daughter and condescend to employ thy skill upon her. O my son, hear the prayer of an old man whose heart is sad, and I will requite thee to the utmost of my means, and Allah, who is more than all of us, will give to thee at the Last Day."

"Where is the girl?" asked the Frank; and the abruptness with which he put the question, deigning no preliminary compliment, caused the bystanders to say among themselves:

"See how rude he is! He must be conscious of very great ability to be thus short with the revered Shems-ud-dìn."

The physician stooped beside the litter.

"O girl, give me thy hand," he said; causing Zeyd and the Circassians to exclaim the more, saying:

"Surely he is a very great physician."

"Let see thy face."

At that Alia uttered a faint scream, and a growl of disapproval came from the four critics.

But Shems-ud-dìn said simply: "Let it be. She is not yet a woman complete, and Allah knows her face at present is not such as to excite desire. Be not afraid, O my dear," he added in a soothing tone to the sufferer. "For thy health's sake, this sacrifice is required of thee."

One glance at the unveiled brow sufficed the foreigner. He rose again quickly and, turning to the sheykh, shrugged his shoulders with an upward look.

"How far have you carried her in this manner?"

"Four days or five, O khawâjah."

For comment the Frank gave another shrug. His face was troubled. The stare of so many eager eyes appeared to irk him.

"She is very near to death," he said at length, half to himself. "Allah alone can cure her now."

Whereupon the listeners whispered: "He knows his trade, this heathen! He makes her case out the worst possible, in order that his skill in curing her may appear the more considerable. Yet is he not totally without religion, for he ascribes the chief power to Allah."

"O sheykh," pursued the Frank, when he had withdrawn beyond earshot of the occupants of the litter, "what can I do? Am I God that thou bringest to me a dying girl, and sayest, 'Heal her'?"

Then Shems-ud-dîn adjured him by the love of Allah, by all things sacred, to have mercy upon Alia, and not to turn away his face from affliction. He said:

"If thou refusest, unto whom, under Allah, can I look for succor? We can but return whence we came, and my girl will die miserably by the roadside, for her strength fails her."

"That is likely," the physician was forced to admit; and the thought seemed to pain him. He frowned and put a hand to his forehead, brushing up his hair beneath the extraordinary form of headdress it pleased him to exhibit. "I cannot receive her in my hospital. It is against the rule, and I am but a servant there. But there is another hospital. Go thither."

Now it was the strength or infirmity of Zeyd ebn Abbâs, when a spectator, to throw himself into any business with a zeal and enthusiasm surpassing that of the transactors. To him, an excited listener, this curt recommendation of another hospital seemed the last word of arrogance. Feeling the call for a supreme effort at persuasion, he snatched up at haphazard certain of the gifts which strewed the pavement, and ran and laid them at the proud one's feet, with such earnestness that an earthen pot, which was among them, cracked upon the stones, releasing a sticky greenish fluid.

"O pig! O clumsy one! Woe is me. Thou hast spilt all my honey. May Allah destroy thy house," roared one of the Circassians, whose present it was.

Then the Frank was seen to smile. O triumph! The Circassians, foremost he whose gift was spoilt, laughed loud for joy of the victory. The Frank smiled; his pride relented; the day was won. To the donor of that honey belonged the glory.

It seemed scarce necessary that the Sheykh Shems-ud-dìn should continue pleading, demonstrating:

"What know I, O hakìm, of another hospital? Is it not enough for us, who are honorable men, to be spurned from the gate of one? Who knows that at the other they will receive the girl, my daughter? The one is for Jews only. It is likely the other will be found to be for Nazarenes only. Thou art a great physician, and thy face is kind. Ah, send us not away! Condescend to treat my child. If she dies, it is from Allah. Do thou but what is in thy power to do, and my blessing on thee. I will pay all thou askest."

Once more the thoughts of the Frank were seen to trouble him. He would not meet the piteous gaze of Shems-ud-dìn, from whose eyes the tears were now streaming.

"Have you a room?" he asked—"a clean room—very clean—one to which air comes freely, where I could visit her daily, and do what I can for her?"

"Merciful Allah! O my son, have I not said that we are strangers in this city. And a room on this pattern were hard to find. We purpose to lodge at a khan beside the Holy Enclosure."

"A khan! It must not be," cried the physician, with more of vehemence than he had hitherto used. "Rather let her remain with the other woman here in my house. And do thou, O sheykh, remain here likewise. As for the others, thy companions, let them go to the khan."

"Now may Allah requite thee, O lord of all kindness!" Shems-ud-dìn raised his tear-stained face to heaven in thanksgiving. "What man of my own faith and nation had done as much for me! May Allah bless thee, exceedingly, and incline thy mind to receive the truth. Thou hast eased me of the heaviest of burdens, for in sooth I was at my wits' end. For myself, I thank thee; I will but stay to see my beloved at rest ere repairing to the khan. Let there be no offense, I entreat thee. I am an old man, O my son, and my habits are a tree above me; I sit in the shade thereof. Moreover, I am a Muslim, and thou, O my son, art a Nazarene. That which seems clean to thee, to me is abomination; and much that I hold sacred seems dirt to thy mind. Let me have but free access to my dear, and may Allah increase thy wealth! Only, I adjure thee, tempt her not to sin with unclean food, and observe all decency in regard to her."

"My doorkeeper is a Muslim. He shall cook for her, if there be any need of cooking, which I think not likely. And the woman with her will doubtless instruct me when I approach her, lest I offend unknowingly."

"May Allah reward thee."

It took Zeyd ebn Abbâs time to realize that the excitement was over. When he did at length grasp the fact, and his mouth shut from gaping, he did not retire with the Circassians. These walked backward to the entry, shouting blessings on the lord of healing; but Zeyd ran and kissed the hem of Shems-ud-dìn's robe.

"O my master," he besought, "let me stay by thee, and go when thou goest. Apart from thee I walk in darkness, I am lost. Thy companions make a mock of me."

"But what of thy donkey?"

"Let it go. Perhaps they will take it to the khan with the rest. I care not greatly though I lose it, for it is borrowed."

To repay the favor shown to him, Zeyd made himself useful. He helped the servants of the house prepare a chamber on the upper floor, and, when that was ready, lent a hand to Mâs and the other negro in carrying the litter up thither. Though cumbrous it was no longer heavy, being eased of the weight of Fatmeh, who now walked beside.

Shems-ud-dìn, alone with Fatmeh, lifted Alia out on the raised Frankish bed prepared for her. The physician had long since gone forth upon the business of his calling. As she sank among the white, soft cushions, she drew a deep sigh. A Nazarene handmaid entered the chamber, bearing milk in a glass, which she offered, saying the master had ordered it.

When Alia, upheld by her father, had drunk of it, she licked her lips and fell back upon the pillows.

"Art content?" whispered Shems-ud-dìn, bending over her.

"It is rest," she murmured faintly, with closed eyes.

CHAPTER IX

It was the third hour after noon when Shems-ud-dìn, by the help of Zeyd ebn Abbâs, made his way to the khan, whither Shibli and the Circassians had gone before. Mâs had begged permission to remain in the house of the Frank, having discovered in the aged doorkeeper a kindred spirit and compatriot. And Shems-ud-dìn was glad to leave him within call of Alia.

At the khan they found two of the Circassians kicking their heels in the dark entry with the mien of unwilling idlers. At sight of Shems-ud-dìn their faces brightened. They asked leave to rejoin their chief, who, with the rest of his men and young Shibli, was gone forth to view the city. They had been left behind only to make report to the sheykh that all was well, and the beasts safely stabled.

"Is my donkey also safe?" asked Zeyd, with more of curiosity than concern.

They answered with a grin: "Be sure of it! The desire of all eyes grinds chaff in the stable here beside thee."

There was no one else in the guest chamber when

Shems-ud-dìn and Zeyd entered. The former took seat upon the diwàn which ran all round the room, and the latter soon followed his example, with care, however, to leave a space between them for reverence. The place got light through the door only. The silence was unbroken save for the buzz of many flies, spasmodical movements on the part of some one in another room, and an occasional far-off neigh from the stable. The faintness and seeming distance of sounds without testified to the thickness of the grimed old walls.

Zeyd, the son of Abbâs, sat gazing at the stonework opposite, now and then risking an awe-stricken glance at his companion's face, which was downcast and very sorrowful. When the lord of the khan came bustling to wish their honors a happy day, Zeyd laid finger to lip, and checked the tide of civilities. The host shuffled off again, disappointed and mystified.

The hue of Shems-ud-dìn's thoughts was indeed very somber. He sat in sackcloth, shamefast before Allah. Where was his faith, his resignation? It had been lost in his eagerness to win the heart of the unbeliever to pity Alia. And his present hope, however faint, was it not an insult to Divine Omnipotence? His soul cried:

"O Lord, I am weak indeed—weaker than I was aware. Strengthen me in the faith. Make me as ready to give up as to receive. Hear my cry out of this shadow, and write not my infirmity against me."

And Zeyd, sitting near him by the wall, and gazing furtively upon his face from time to time, thought:

"Was there ever such a saint? Surely he is holiest of all men living! Surely angels talk with him, and the Most High leads him by the hand. O happy me, to sit unrebuked by the side of such an one, the companion of his musing!"

They had sat thus in silence a long while, when footsteps rang without with the noise of something clanking along the flags. The voice of the host rose shrill in an ecstacy of salutation. The next minute his burly form passed the doorway, ushering with profound salaams a Turkish officer in full uniform.

"His Excellency Abd-ur-Rahman Bey seeks audience of the illustrious Sheykh Shems-ud-dìn," he announced with unction, a perceptible increase of respect in his tone.

In contrast with his constraint of that morning, Abd-ur-Rahman came forward now with outstretched arms and fell on his father's neck. Zeyd, the son of Abbâs, stood bowing awhile, but, gaining no notice by his mute obeisance, went out to gossip with the lord of the khan. Abd-ur-Rahman scowled after him.

"Who is that person, O my father?" he asked with fastidious lips.

"It is a good, poor man, a friend of mine, who accompanies me for love, not gain, yet waits upon my needs like a servant. I recommend him to thy favor, O my son."

Abd-ur-Rahman laughed, between amusement and vexation.

"Thou wast ever addicted to strange friendships, O my father. Remember the begging Hâj who came years ago to our house and dwelt there many months in thy love, laughing in his beard. He persuaded thee without a vestige of proof that he was a Hâfiz and most pious, while the town without soon knew him for a drunkard and a cheat, and Hassan Agha drove him forth at the last. When wilt thou learn to distinguish? By my head, I would do much to avoid being seen in the company of him who has just left us; and lo! thou hast sworn brotherhood with him."

Shems-ud-dìn shook his head archly. "It is plain to see, O my dear, in what school thou hast studied. I hear my brother's voice in every word."

Abd-ur-Rahman smiled. "That may be. But say, O my father, wilt thou not take a little thought for appearances? Out there, in the wilderness, it matters nothing, for all men know thee. But here, in the city, it is different. Here men judge of men with the eyes only; and when one does anything uncommon, there springs up a talk about it, which is not pleasant. It distressed me, at our meeting this morning, to behold thee in so outlandish a company. They are good, faithful men, and our friends, that is known. And perhaps any one of them, seen separately, might pass unheeded. But all together. . . . As well cry aloud in the market! Already the tale of your arrival is noised abroad; and the mouth of rumor is a dirty fountain; it adds something foul to what it utters. Men speak of thee as a madman, of thy companions as mockers at thy madness. They say that thou hast left thy daughter, my sister, in the power of a certain Frank, a man unmarried and but lately come to the city, of whom nothing is known. Surely that is an idle tale, O my father?"

"It is truth, though the wrong side thereof. Thy sister is not alone. Fatmeh and Mâs are beside her in that house. Moreover, I have gazed on the face of the Frank, and found it a good face. They assure me he is a clever physician. It is enough."

"Verily thou hast a talent for liking strange beasts. At the least, O my father, go not abroad with our Circassian friends in a body as you rode to-day. The tongue of the city defames and sullies; and I, thy son, enjoy some standing here, and a name not unrespected."

"In all which I hear plainly the voice of my brother Milhem—the dear one. How is his health in these days?"

"He is well, the praise to Allah! In everyone of his letters he charges me with some fond message unto thee, O my father."

"How comes it that I have received none of them? Why hast thou not written to me these many months? Is there any dearth of travelers in our direction that thou couldst not send me word by one of them?"

The young Bey hung his head, examining the hilt of his sword as though there had been something amiss with it. He stammered:

"Since I came to this city, I have been very busy acquiring proficiency in my new duties. And in the evening, when I have leisure, I am weary; and to write, unless by daylight, hurts my eyes. I have sinned, O my father."

"I forgive and bless thee. But, ah me! how like thou growest to my brother Milhem." The sheykh put hand to forehead and indulged his memory a little space. Then, turning sharply to his son, "Thou hast not asked concerning the health of Alia."

"How is her condition?" said Abd-ur-Rahman promptly.

"Praise Allah for the kindness of that Frankish doctor. . . . Thou wilt come to-morrow and visit her in his house?"

Abd-ur-Rahman shook his head and smiled deprecatingly.

"That may scarcely be, O my father. My position in El Cûds is one of some prominence. I dare not invite scandal by entering a house of unbelief; about which, in connection with thee and thy friends, there is talk enough already. . . . Tell me, O my father, why dost thou take so much trouble on account of the illness of my sister? Wouldst thou have done as much for the health of me, thy son? It is said that thou hast promised half thy fortune to this Frank. And yet a man is held of more account than a girl. They dub thee madman, O my father. I love not to hear such insolent talk of thee."

"Thou canst always smite the mouth of the speaker," began Shems-ud-dìn, indignant. But before he could proceed, heavy footsteps sounded in the entry, and Hassan burst in.

"O my eyes, I have seen two Bedawis of that

same band which we passed yesterday upon the road. They were prowling near the castle, entering into conversation with the soldiers. By Allah, I know their business at the Feast of the Nazarenes. They would steal rifles——"

"Ah, of a truth, would they?" said Abd-ur-Rahman dryly.

"Ha, is it thou, Abd-ur-Rahman, O child of my soul? By Allah, in the dimness I mistook thy form for that of our glorious Zeyd ebn Abbâs. A mercy thou didst speak. How is thy health, O beloved? In sh' Allah, it is the best possible. Thou art come, doubtless, to rejoice with thy father. There is no longer any fear for Alia. She is safe in the care of an English physician."

"I must depart," said the Bey soon after, when more footsteps echoed without. "Be not wroth with me, O my father, if during the course of thy sojourn here I shall appear sometimes neglectful. Thou knowest not how fettered is the life of one in authority."

Shems-ud-dìn accompanied his son as far as the outer portal of the khan, a low arch open on a narrow shadowed way. Overhead, above the square-cut roofs, the sky was flushed with sunset. At parting, Shems-ud-dìn took the lad's face between his two hands and, looking straight into his eyes, said quietly:

"Of a truth, in speech and manner thou art grown the very marrow of my brother Milhem. He could never perceive the ground of my doings. My heart is sad at present—very sad; so I entreat thee not to vex my understanding with every idle rumor which may wound thy vanity. I am answerable to none save Allah for my madness. Now go thy way, and may Allah keep thee always."

With that he kissed his son between the eyebrows and let him go.

CHAPTER X

THE sun rode high above the Holy City, but a freshness of the dawn still lurked in the shade of her rough walls, in the gloom of her covered ways, which swarmed with people in all kinds of raiment representative of every nation under heaven. To anyone threading that crowded labyrinth of whitish stone, ancient and coherent, glimpses of the pure blue sky became welcome as a flower on rocks. For Shems-ud-dìn, accustomed through so many years to wide horizons and an open road, the overshadowing walls made a prison. The hubbub of the bazaars dazed him, and he felt hurt by the careless shouldering of other wayfarers.

He had been to visit Alia, and was making his way, under guidance of the faithful Zeyd, to the Sacred Area, when he met Shibli walking with Hassan Agha and his attendant Circassians amid the throng in a long, dim market.

" How is the health of our dove this morning? " cried Hassan, speaking for them all. " In sh' Allah, the poor one is much better? "

"If not better, her frame has rest—for which Allah be praised!" returned Shems-ud-dìn. "The people of the house are very kind, as I learn from the mouth of Mâs. The Lord reward them! . . . O Shibli, son of my hope, unless thou hast some grave business, come with me to the Dome of the Rock, whither I go to pray. It is long since I spoke with thee in private. Come and let thy voice comfort me, O my dear."

Shibli obeyed, as in duty bound; but his face often turned to gaze wistfully after the Circassians, and the lines of his mouth expressed grievance.

"Is the health of the beloved indeed no better?" he felt it incumbent on him to ask.

"I know not how to answer thee, O my son. I fear hope as a friend untried. It is enough to desire. Notwithstanding, if Allah wills that she be made whole, there appears to my mind a possibility which yesterday I could not discern."

"Praise be to Allah!" murmured Shibli very properly.

The quiet of the Muslim quarter brought refreshment to Shems-ud-dìn, after the clamor of the motley throng in the bazaars. Old walls rose high on either hand. Jutting lattices, with here and there an arch, encroached on the jewel sky. In the shade of one ancient portal, ornate but crumbling to decay, sat a breadseller asleep behind two tiers of flat, brown loaves. A man with a water skin on his back turned in at the doorway of a house before them. A grave notable, in apparel sober but rich, passed them without a glance, one hand in his breast. Everything in that dim, once splendid quarter told of a proud reserve, of a dignity that needs no trump for its assertion. The air was sad with the sadness of great things past.

They entered what seemed a disused bazaar of rare magnificence, a huge corridor with a lofty vaulted roof, which got light from the far end where its tall arch framed the sky. The place was deserted and ruinous, its floor uneven and strewn with the brash of masonry. Shems-ud-dìn quickened step instinctively to gain the light which picked out the faces of his companions from the shades wherein they had walked so long.

The outer sunshine crashed on their sight with the splinter of a thousand lances. The great mouth of the passage yawned black as night behind them. On either side of it ran a high irregular wall, bearing here and there a lattice, the end of the houses in this direction. They stood on a strip of clear ground, on which a few old trees cast blots of shadow; a place waste, save for patches of wrought pavement and certain small, domed shrines as delicate as toys of ivory.

Before them, at no great distance, rose a flight of wide steps leading up on to a terraced plateau, and at a point farther off up sprang a sister flight exactly similar. On the top of either stairway, in the gate of the Haram, stood three slender columns, light and graceful as flower stems, supporting arches. At one end of the plateau, seen through cypress trees, crouched a mosque of many aisles; and numberless small, domed buildings—shrines and cells and pulpits—capped the terrace walls. But what drew and absorbed their gaze to the forgetting of all else, the sun and center of all, was a mighty dome, in form and color somewhat resembling a ripe fig, springing from the roof of an octagon of two kinds of marble, wrought together into cunning patterns. Not a foot of the great building but had been treated minutely, curiously, by the hands of forgotten craftsmen. In the full light of morning, there in that sand-hued place, it bloomed a wondrous iris of the hills, a thing to wring a shout from the dying.

Even Shibli forgot his dudgeon, and joined reverently with Zeyd ebn Abbâs in reciting the prayer of first approach, after Shems-ud-dìn.

Then, having gazed all about them, they crossed the waste ground and mounted the steps. Discarding slippers, they passed along a time-worn pavement to the place of washing. With the exception of two middle-aged men in dark robes and white turbans, who sat disputing gravely beneath a tree and gave but one look to the pilgrims, they seemed alone in the vast inclosure.

When, having purified their bodies, they ventured to approach the Noble Sanctuary, Shems-ud-dìn thought well to remind them of its claims to reverence.

" Within, beneath this admirable dome," he said, " we shall behold the rock whereon Neby Ibrahìm, the Friend of God, prepared to sacrifice his beloved son Ismaìl, at the bidding of the Most High. Hither also, in an after age, was our lord Muhammed, the Apostle of God, borne by night on the celestial beast, Burac; and from that same rock was he transported to the seventh heaven, being yet mortal. Surely there is no stone in all the world, save only that of Mekka, more worthy of our reverence than this rock, which God has hallowed from of old. And the Khalif, Omar El Khattab (peace to him), did well to raise this splendid dome above it."

Zeyd ebn Abbâs devoured those high words

greedily. Shibli heard them with respect. At the entrance to the Dome of the Rock, Shems-ud-dìn ceased speaking, and they passed into the tinted gloom of the sanctuary.

While Shibli and Zeyd ebn Abbâs paced the ring of pavement, studying the texts worked in mosaic upon the walls and above the arches, looking on the natural rock so gloriously enshrined, Shems-ud-dìn knelt and made prostration, praying:

"O Allah, pardon! Grant to thy servant faith on the pattern of El Khalìl, who in this place offered his dearest freely unto thee. Am I not the very opposite of Neby Ibrahìm El Khalìl? When all reasonable means failed to restore my child, and prayer had been made in vain, Thy Will was manifest to me. Yet I presumed to seek other aid, I sought to procure her health by man's exertion. I followed the contrivance of my own mind. Am I not impious, therefore? Am I not abominable? What am I that Thou shouldst hear me, or my deeds upon the earth to make a claim upon Thee? Nevertheless, Thou deignest to give ear to the prayers of men, and hast ordained prayer unto us as an offering pleasing in Thy sight. Hear me, O Lord, in this my extremity! Oh, have mercy on my daughter, the innocent; and smite me rather, for I am sinful! And whatever Thy Will concerning her, teach me to resign myself to it utterly. Subdue my mind and my soul, and lead me in the way of the upright."

He rose at length from off the pavement, and went and sat crosslegged, his back against the wall. Tears blinded him. The footsteps of Shibli and Zeyd echoed in the vast dome, and their whispering made a hollow murmur. But Shems-ud-dìn heard nothing save the clamor of his inward strife.

All at once a voice near his ear said, "Why weepest thou, O my brother?"

With a start, as one awakes out of sleep, he looked and beheld one in flowing raiment standing before him, a very old man who leaned upon a staff. His face was deeply furrowed where the white hair grew not, and his lips were shriveled and sucked inward as when the gums beneath have shrunken, being toothless. Shems-ud-dìn sat amazed by the apparition, for he had not heard the old man's steps approaching nor the tap of his staff along the stones. He saw the forms of Zeyd and Shibli afar off, standing watching as men smitten with dismay.

"What ails thee, O my brother? Wherefore weepest thou? I cannot discern thy likeness, for my eyes grow dim; but I see thy beard white as my own, and I hear thy sobs. What dire distress is thine, an old man inured to human griefs, that thou so lamentest?"

"A long story, O my brother."

"A long story is the best of stories, and I like it none the worse for promising to be sad. At my age one is impatient only of abruptness, the inconsequence of the merry and light-minded. Lend me the help of thy hand, O my brother, that I may compose my limbs to sit beside thee."

Shems-ud-dìn reached forth his hand and the old man grasped it, steadying himself therewith while he tucked his staff beneath his left elbow. He was about to subside upon the bare stones, when Zeyd ebn Abbâs darted forward and spread his ragged cloak upon the ground beneath him. The old man smiled vaguely, exposing his toothless gums.

"May Allah requite thee, O my son! May this thy courtesy be counted to thee for righteousness! Thy cloak is old and of poor material, as my hands perceive. May a rich mantle fall upon thee from the hand of Allah!"

Zeyd bowed his head to the blessing, and rejoined Shibli with a face of great elation.

"Now deign to impart thy story, O my brother!" said the old man, when fairly seated.

Shems-ud-dìn complied straightway. He abated

nothing of his own frowardness, but confessed it throughout the story, speaking much of his soul's uneasiness on that account.

At the end, there was silence for a little space. Then that old man spoke:

"During all the years that I have been Chief of the Learned in this place, never—Allah witness!—never heard I such a tale as this thou hast related. Beloved, I see not with thy eyes; I see goodness everywhere in thy conduct, save only in the one point of thy recourse to the unbeliever, of which thou madest naught in the telling. This Frank is not an infidel like another infidel. He is of those who openly oppose the faith. Is there not a korân concerning such an one: 'The worst beasts in God's sight are those who are obstinate unbelievers'?"

"But, on the other hand, there is also this korân: 'Allah is our Lord and your Lord; unto us our works, and unto you your works; no quarreling between us and you; for Allah will gather in us both, and unto Him we shall return.'"

"Good. But that word is abrogated in the judgment of all the learned!"

"Not of all, by thy leave! There be many who assert that no word from Allah can be rendered null, that this has its season, and that its season, but all are eternally valid. I was ever of the party of these last. As to the degree of intercourse permissible with unbelievers, and more especially with the People of the Book, it is nowhere fixed for us. I could quote a hundred traditions in support of either argument, and the best precedents are in like manner at variance. For instance, if we refer to the Sûnna——"

"Stay! Hast thou studied the Sûnna?"

"Assuredly; and all our commentators and, I verily believe, every scripture relevant to the subject."

"O happy day for me! Welcome, and again welcome, O my soul! Deign now to dispute a little! It is seldom I can exercise my learning; very seldom I am able to confer with a man like thee. The lamp of knowledge does but smoke nowadays."

It was long since Shems-ud-dìn had enjoyed conversation with his equal in learning. The two sheykhs held long conference, while Zeyd sat on his heels watching them, and Shibli wandered to and fro, yawning frequently and viewing the wonders about him with a growing disenchantment.

At last the old man rose by the help of Shems-ud-dìn and the attentive Zeyd. He said:

"My peace on thee! Thou art a prince of scholars, and a man most righteous. If I perceive any fault in thee, it is that thy mind exalts small matters, and overlooks or belittles points of real importance—a common failing among us learned in the Law, professed quibblers. This matter of thy going to the Frank is, to my thinking, no trifle. I hope to convince thee of the wrong in it at some other time. Come hither whenever thou art so minded; it is a boon I crave of thee. Ask for Mahmûd Ali, which is my name. And if ever thou desirest to pray alone, there stand cells enough within our precincts, empty, for the most part, save in Ramadan, which is not yet. They and all I dispose of are thine to use, O my soul's brother!"

With a parting benison the old man hobbled away, bowed upon his staff.

Shems-ud-dìn said one last prayer, then went out with his companions into the blinding sunlight.

Zeyd, the son of Abbâs, raised his hands on high, toward that sapphire dome which has the world for pavement. In a loud voice he praised Allah, and blessed the day on which it had been given him to witness the meeting of two most holy men, and garner in his imagination a drop or two of the celestial wisdom that had gushed in rivers from their mouths.

Shibli drew breath of relief, and looked upon the heaped-up, whitish city with a lover's eyes.

CHAPTER XI

"COME, O my brothers! Talk is vain when the throat is dry and the belly empty. Lead the way to some place where we can eat together, and drink a cup or two of good coffee. So shall our business prosper by the blessing of Allah."

"But we have no money, O my lord! How should we soldiers have money, seeing they never pay us?"

"With me is money enough. Deign to eat and drink at my expense, and mine the honor."

"May Allah Most High repay your noble Excellency!"

Two soldiers of a rank somewhat above the private, accosted by Hassan Agha amid the crowd in a long bazaar, laid hand to breast and lip and brow, bowing to his invitation as men too greatly honored. Their tongues still wagged of reluctance and unworthiness even while their feet made speed toward the place of refreshment. Three Circassians, the companions of Hassan's morning prowl, followed intelligently like trained hounds. Shibli went along with them, mystified yet admiring.

The tavern to which they came was chill and dark within. They carried their stools to the wide entrance, where they could enjoy the relative warmth and light of the street without.

"Arac, O lord of good cheer! Bring to us arac!" cried the soldiers.

"Allah forbid!" murmured Shibli with a start, gazing in horror at those reckless ones. He knew only that they called for a fiery drink and maddening, accounted poison by all faithful men.

Thereupon the whole company burst out laughing, and the tavern keeper, attendant on their needs, laughed with them, holding his belly.

"Allah forgive our ribaldry!" said Hassan. "The sin is ours, not his. Know, O my brothers, that this is a good, virtuous youth, the disciple of a certain holy one revered of all. Allah witness, and do thou take note, O Shibli, that I, for my part, touch not the abomination. Neither I nor my companions; let it be told the sheykh!" He turned then to the soldiers, adding, "It behooves a man to avoid small offenses when he has the uncommon honor to be the friend and companion of the holiest of living men. And that honor is upon all of us here."

The soldiers expressed their polite interest in tones of commiseration. To sip their arac without reproach, they had taken seat close to a pillar of the doorway which screened them, when they leant to drink, from the gaze of the passer-by.

"Once, when I was a boy," said one of them, entertaining Shibli and the rest, while his colleague spoke aside with Hassan, "I had the honor to lie down beneath the horse of a holy sheykh—I and my father and my big brother and a thousand more. It was in El Bica'a, behind Lebanon. The plain was strewn with living bodies. You could not see the ground anywhere between us. Then the sheykh rode his horse over the backs of us, and when it came to my back, lo, it was to me no more than if some girl, mistress of beauty, fondled me for love, there where the hoof pressed. And the spot has been blessed ever since; for when I do evil it pains me, and when I do good it is again as if some hand of love caressed me. By Allah, it pains me now for the sake of this arac—a sin, as the youth rightly declared! . . . A strange thing—not so, O my masters?

"I remember to have seen, in Anadol far from here, a man who went well-nigh naked, his face like the earth itself for dirt and roughness. A one-eyed man might see that he was holy above the rest of us.

That man leaned upon a sword—upon the blade of it, by Allah! so that the point came forth at his back. Then he drew it out slowly, showing all men how the blood rained from it. As for him, he laughed to see the red stuff fall. Then, as we looked for him to die, he began to dance, chanting praise to Allah. And that he did not once nor twice, but many times before he died. Strange things are seen in the world, O my masters! By Allah, I count you fortunate! I myself would fain behold that saint of yours. Peradventure he would grant me to witness some marvel worth relating, like the turning of wicked people into dogs. . . ."

"The Sheykh Shems-ud-dìn is no wandering derwish, whose mind is to cajole the vulgar," broke in Shibli, from the height of indignation. "He is a learned sheykh of the religion, a man of high lineage and great wealth, to whose wisdom even princes defer with reverence."

"Ma sh' Allah!" smiled the soldier, but little impressed. "Your talk had led me to suppose him otherwise. Why call him saint, then? Has he wrought no signs in the land?"

"Of a truth, that has he, by Allah," said Hassan, who had ended his whispered conference. "He brought light to the city where we dwell. He is lord of the jân. They have had no master like him since the death of Suleyman the Wise. When his daughter fell ill, and all help failed, it was by advice of a jinni, his slave, that he brought her hither, to this city, to the house of a Frank physician, where she now lies. Signs, say you? I assure you, by Allah, he is lord of them all! He knows the language of beasts, and on our way hither made use of that knowledge to restore to a certain poor fellâh his camel, which had been long lost. The fellâh, his name Zeyd ebn Abbâs, is still with us. If thou wilt, thou canst speak with him and hear the wondrous story from his own lips."

"Is it truth thou speakest?" asked one of the soldiers, with a shrug aside to his mate.

"By Allah, it is truth! All these are witnesses with me. Ask one of them. Ask any man acquainted with his holiness!"

They sat a-row in the wide archway, brushed by the raiment of the throng without, hearing snatches of conversation, shouts, laughter, and the ceaseless shuffle of feet along the stones; while at their backs was darkness, save for one red gleam of fire, which the ample form of the taverner kept eclipsing as it revolved in his avocations about the brazier.

"Allah knows I should count it an honor to behold that saint of yours," said one of the soldiers at length, in a manner of resolution.

"And I also," agreed the other in the same tone of belated conviction.

"That is easy. If Allah will, we shall find him without difficulty."

"Let us go, then!"

"Slowly, slowly, O my two dear ones!" Hassan's face turned cunning in the mold of thought. "Is our business settled quite? No, I think not so. We have not yet appointed an hour for the transaction. Let it be after to-morrow, toward the fifth hour of night. What say you?"

The soldiers shook their heads.

"No," said each, upon reflection. "After to-morrow is the great feast of the Nazarenes—of half of them, that is to say; for the two halves quarrel so that they cannot even keep festival upon the same day. . . . It is the busiest of the year for us. We shall stop their fighting in the church; and after that, it is likely, we shall be called upon to keep order in the streets of the city. It is work enough for one day. Let our business stand over till the night beyond."

"As you will," said Hassan, playing indifference. "But I would have the goods as soon as possible. My eyes have perceived certain rascals in the garb of the

Bedawi prowling near the castle and whispering with you soldiers. Now, I adjure you, face the matter! View it fairly with clean eyes! Are we not—my men and I—loyal servants of the Sultàn appointed from of old to guard the Eastern portals of this land, and so entitled to arms and ammunition like you others? As for the Bedû, what are they? Marauders, thieves, murderers—Allah knows them! It were a crime to give them the preference!"

The soldiers exchanged sly glances, swift as sword thrusts. Said one of them, cringing, "What sayest thou, O Excellency? The Bedû! . . . Allah pity! What Bedû?"

"Perchance," thrust in the other with an air of extreme candor, "our good lord would allude to certain tribesmen who, calling themselves Catholics, are come up to fight at the feast."

Hassan laughed. "Think not I trust you. Remember only that, in the place where I dwell, it is counted death to offend Hassan Agha. . . . And now, unless your desire is changed, we will show you the saint of whom we talked but now."

"With joy and alacrity," replied the soldiers.

All, rising, kicked back their stools. They smiled one to another, showing white teeth, as they yawned and stretched themselves. Hassan told some small gleaming coins into the grimed hand of the tavverner, thrust out in anticipation from the inner gloom.

Suddenly, with a muttered exclamation not of blessing, the soldiers dodged behind the stone doorpost. The hindmost, upsetting a stool, cursed its religion as it fell. In the covered way without, they had seen a young officer riding upon a black horse, slowly, because of the crowd. It was Abd-ur-Rahman Bey.

Hassan Agha stood forward with a jaunty air, a hand on his white mustache.

"Hail, O sun of soldiery! May thy day be happy, O child of a blessed birth! Deign to dismount and drink one cup of coffee with him who first taught thee to handle sword and gun!"

His design in thus shouting before the multitude was simply to vex the false pride of the son of Shems-ud-dìn. It amazed him to have his salutation returned twofold, to see the proud youth alight and give his horse to a bystander.

"How is thy health, O Hassan, light of my eyes?" inquired Abd-ur-Rahman, smiling, as they touched hands. "And thou, O Shibli: is all well with thee? . . . How is Alia? How the dear old man?"

He chose for seat one of those stools which the soldiers had just vacated, next to that which was overturned. Straightway he became aware of a shuffling close at hand, and, looking round the doorpost, beheld two of his own men.

"What is this, O Muhammed—O Rashìd?" he asked, smiling. "Is my face this morning so terrible that you must hide from it? Come forth, O foolish ones, and attend me to the castle, whither I go presently. . . . O Hassan, a word with thee in private, by thy leave!"

He carried his stool into the inner gloom, and Hassan followed him. They conversed apart until the coffee was served, when they brought back their stools into the light of the doorway. Hassan reappeared frowning, but the countenance of the young caïd beamed, as before, of an imperturbable good humor.

Abd-ur-Rahman stayed but to swallow a cupful of coffee; then rose, smiling on the company, and took leave. The two soldiers followed him with the demeanor of whipped curs. They went forward to offer him assistance at mounting his horse, and he availed himself of their obsequiousness, still smiling.

"Ma sh' Allah," muttered Hassan, as he watched them depart. "To reflect that it is but a youth, one whom yesterday I held upon my knee. By the Lord of Heaven and Earth, he is a devil! . . . That is not the son of the Sheykh Shems-ud-dìn! It is the son of Milhem Pasha, Eblìs in person——!"

As they sauntered forth in search of the sheykh, he continued:

"May it please you, he forbids us to touch a rifle. He says that he will apply to the authorities on our behalf for a special grant. The praise to Allah! We shall wait a hundred years and see never a cartridge! Our need is instant, and if we get not the things, others less worthy will presently obtain them. I know these outlying garrisons. At Istanbûl or Edreyneh it may be different. But for Esh-Shâm, El Cûds, Haleb, there is one way in all of them."

He ceased not to growl in soliloquy.

They had entered a narrow alley of the Muslim quarter, strolling as their manner was, when there came a sound of feet hurrying after, and a ragged soldier overtook them, sweating and out of breath.

"Say, is not one among you the excellent Hassan Agha, whom Allah preserve?"

"I am he."

The man louted. "A word from the Bimbashi Muhammed—he that had charge of the armory (Allah witness how I ran to overtake thee, questioning all men as I ran; for I had but a hint of thy likeness and the number of thy companions from him who sent me)—a word from the Bimbashi Muhammed which he whispered to me in the castle yard as he went to durance: 'Attempt nothing, for the love of Allah! Lay aside thy purpose. For things are not as of wont.' "

"Good. I thank thee." Hassan bestowed on the man a coin and received his blessing in exchange. He appeared unmoved by the tidings.

"The day wears on," he said. "Let us go at once to the sheykh, for I am impatient to hear his news."

"At this hour we shall find him in the Haràm," asserted Shibli, who was supposed to know.

Toward the sanctuary they went accordingly. It had thundered in the night; the day had dawned in rain, and so continued until the third hour. But now the clouds were rolled away to eastward. As the little group emerged from the buried ways of the city on to the open ground below the shrine, Omar's dome was a dew-drenched flower in the sunlight, the scattered cypress trees pricked a sky of dreamy blue.

At the top of the steps, along the edge of the noble terrace, rose divers little cubic buildings like to tombs. Their open arches gave the effect of mouths gaping on the central dome.

On the threshold of one of those alcoves, gazing raptly in, squatted Zeyd, the son of Abbâs. The fellâh laid a finger to his lip at their approach.

"Hush!" he whispered and pointed. There, in the white recess, sat Shems-ud-dìn, stiffly rocking to and fro, his face set, his eyes steadfastly downcast. "The health of the girl is worse to-day. She knew him not. Let Allah comfort him!"

All murmured of compassion and reverence. Shibli threw himself down beside Zeyd, in the same shadow with his master. The rest sat on their heels in the sunshine, enjoying that sight of holiness.

CHAPTER XII

SHEMS-UD-DÌN now divided his days between the house of the physician and that tomblike cell; and the two scenes overlapped and obscured one another, becoming confounded in his imagination. In those days his thoughts but brushed our earth as with the skirt of an outer robe. The Angels of Life and Death were his elect companions. When, repairing at nightfall to the khan, he descried known faces, met the outcry of condolence, it was with the blindness of a sun gazer, with the deafness of one long a stranger to men's talk.

Yet, even in the deep of anguish there were moments when he saw and heard; and those moments showered gold in the lap of Zeyd ebn Abbâs, his doglike attendant. They repaid the hours which the whilom owner of a playful camel had spent in silence at his feet; the times when, unthanked, unperceived, Zeyd had guided his master's steps through the crowd.

These brief communings with his lord, which were all the wages of Zeyd, took place generally at the cell on the edge of the close, where Shems-ud-dìn seemed most content. The fellâh too loved that spot above all others of the city. Squatting in the sunshine of that holy place, near by a world-famed shrine, himself the guardian of a saint, he was conscious of laying up a store of sanctity, of pious memories, to sustain him through the rest of life. When the aged Mahmûd Ali came, as often happened, to observe and bemoan the sad case of a fellow-sage, he never failed to bless Zeyd and praise his fidelity. So that that simple man cried in his soul:

"How great my happiness! Behold, I grow daily in goodness, without effort, even as flowers grow, through converse with such holy ones. They scorn me not as do the Circassians, who, therefore, it is well seen, are but low people."

At the house of the Frank physician, while Shems-ud-dìn remained in the sick room, Zeyd was accustomed to sit with Mâs and Ismaìl the doorkeeper in the little court. But the two old negroes were not instructive; their happiness consisted in holding one another's hand and smiling foolishly. Zeyd's mind, apt to wander from such converse, hung in danger from the charms of a barefaced serving woman, who kept crossing and recrossing the court—of set purpose, he supposed, to entice him. Only by the mercy of Allah did he escape the daily snare of her. As the companion of a great saint, he had taken the pilgrim's vow of total abstinence.

On an evening when Zeyd sat thus resisting temptation in the company of old Mâs (the doorkeeper having gone forth to drink the air and display a new garment, gift of the Frank his master), Shems-ud-dìn came down from the place of sickness, showing a countenance far brighter than he was wont to bear.

The two arose and, bowing, put their question; to which he replied:

"The praise to Allah! This morning I dared not rejoice, but this evening, seeing the improvement still maintained, I render thanks to God. Come, O Zeyd, O Mâs, walk with me a little in the streets of the city. Let us view the much merchandise and the throng of men, for my soul is glad within me."

Upon that Mâs, seeing his master's soul at ease, ventured upon a petition he had long borne it in his mind to make. Stooping, he touched the hem of Shems-ud-dìn's robe, then kissed the hand which had touched it. He exclaimed:

"Deign to hear me, O my lord! I ask a favor —a small thing, far beneath thee. There dwell here in the city many poor men, servants, black like me. These meet together privately to be judged of their sheykh, who is no other than Ismaìl, the doorkeeper at this house. They seek the right, but as the street dogs seek, whom no man stoops to feed. Their prayer is through me unto thee, O my master, that thou wilt grant them a little instruction. This is the Day of Assembly, when they meet always toward sunset. Vouchsafe to honor them, and I, thy slave, will guide thee to the place."

"With pleasure and alacrity," replied Shems-ud-dìn, and the teeth of the negro gleamed forth in satisfaction.

Forthwith, at his accustomed mooning pace, Mâs set about his preparations. From out a vault, whereof the door stood open, he produced a lantern, which he opened to be sure the candle was not spent. He put a box of Frankish matches within the frame, shut to the glass, and, taking a staff that leaned against the wall, smiled of readiness.

Zeyd, with Shems-ud-dìn, followed him out into the streets, where forms moved vaguely in rich lights and shadows, like the concourse of a dream.

Zeyd raised his eyes to the sky, a blue eye of love perusing the sun-red city, and his thoughts were a lump in his throat. At length men recognized the holiness of the Sheykh Shems-ud-dìn; at last they cried to him for light. Surely Allah had smitten the multitude with blindness; certainly the notables of this city, her merchants, her high officials were as blind as their own walls. Allah had put out their eyes, as He had put out those of Hassan Agha the iniquitous and his crew of reprobates. It had been reserved for a poor fellâh, for a few low negroes, to perceive and welcome the blessing from on high.

They crossed the open space before the tower, where was noise and much people, shadows in an amber glow, and thence passed by dim and quiet ways through the Armenian quarter. Here and there, along the coping of old walls, the leaves of stone plants burned like tongues of flame. A gate yawned on them suddenly, its square tower red in the stream of sunset. It let them out on to the brink of a gorge full of dusty gloom.

Mâs kept to the top of the rocks, close along by the foot of the wall. Following, through deep shadows, Zeyd in mind compared himself to one proved faithful passing, by support of the Prophet, over the hair bridge into Paradise. Between black wall and blue abyss, their path ran, a very thread. The ravines seemed fathomless. The high hills were of the sky, all warmth. The features of the landscape were transfigured, exaggerated, made monstrous with excess of color like an opium dream. Yet though he felt as one poised in mid-air, Zeyd knew no fear; having with him the saint, that enchanter whose mere neighborhood made a seer of the poor fellâh.

At a turn of the wall, Mâs waited for them to overtake him. There a wide prospect was revealed. Far away, across a darkling sea of ridge and gully, stood a pile all rosy in the sun's last rays. It was the rampart of their own wild land, which frowns at dawn upon the Sea of Lot. Shems-ud-dìn stood still to gaze upon that distant splendor. But Mâs plucked his robe.

"Behold the assembly, O my master!"

The stretch of embattled wall seemed of iron, bounding a hearth of colored fires. It cast such gloom upon the rocks, that Zeyd must look twice ere he discerned the white of turbans and men's raiment near at hand.

"Great honor is on all of you!" cried Mâs, as he moved on. A group of men, set in circle upon a grass-clad crown of rock beneath the wall, rose as one and did obeisance with words of blessing.

"Pursue your business, I entreat you," said Shems-ud-dìn graciously, taking seat with them. "Let not my presence trouble you. I would listen awhile before I speak."

After some polite demur, the blacks resumed their

conference; and Shems-ud-dìn listened with interest, but the mind of Zeyd turned again to the contemplation of its own blessedness.

One of the circle, who was called the Pearl, told with much childish lamentation how he had been wrongfully accused of theft, and beaten by his master. "I know well the thief," he blubbered. "And my back is sore. I would see him punished. Is it right that I inform my master?"

Then their head, that was the doorkeeper of the Frank physician, stroked his beard and answered thoughtfully:

"To steal is not good. Where I was born, they cut off the right hand of him who steals. But here it is otherwise. Here be many thieves, very wicked men. . . . Inform not against thy fellow-servant, now that thy trial is past. In the moment of pain it had been well enough to name him. Thou art young, O Pearl, and strong, none like thee. Take that thief apart, and beat him even as thou wast beaten, that he sin no more."

When the negroes ceased to praise God for that wise judgment, another cause was brought forward. But Zeyd heard no more. Watching the blush fade upon those distant heights, the wall of his own land, he sat entranced by the mystery of being.

The buzz of voices ceased. He heard as if in a dream the voice of Ismaìl say:

"Deign now to instruct us, O master!"

"It is I who have received instruction, O thou Locman of this age," replied Shems-ud-dìn; and the tones of his voice unclosed Zeyd's consciousness, like the sun's touch on a flower. "Allah is with you simple ones. Verily the mercy of Allah is the free spring of the poor."

And he continued speaking of the mercy of Allah in such splendid terms that Zeyd caught fire at them and seemed inspired, he also crying: "Hear him!" "O Allah!" "O Lord!" "His mouth is gold!" "Praise to Allah!" "I faint!" "I die!" moaning and sighing gustily like one possessed.

The end of the speech was for Zeyd like a dazed awakening. He saw the negroes rise, a dark mass, and heard them praise Allah for that grand discourse. Then he saw Mâs with the lantern lighted, and thereby knew that it was night and time to move.

The light danced and wavered before him, a thing unreal. They were back in the heart of the city ere he knew they had passed the gate. Mâs and the sheykh of the negroes stalked on ahead, the lantern between them. Zeyd himself followed close upon Shems-ud-dìn. All at once he remembered that they were going now to the khan, to the companions, and a sudden jealousy inflamed him.

He said, "O my master, where is the youth Shibli, thy disciple? This day makes the second that he has not been near thee. He grows bad with the Circassians, who set their minds to corrupt him."

"Hassan Agha has much business. And it is natural that Shibli should desire to see the city in his company."

"And thy son. May Allah guard me from begetting one like him. Since the day of our arrival he has not once visited thee."

"Doubtless he has been at the khan in my absence."

"Not so, for I have made inquiry."

"He has his duties, and the pleasures of his age. He is young, I am old. In distress I ask no company save thine, O kind one!"

"May Allah requite thee, O my dear lord!"

At the house of the Frank, Shems-ud-dìn entered with the negroes for the purpose of complimenting the physician upon the improvement wrought in Alia. After a very little while he rejoined Zeyd, who at once felt a change in his demeanor.

"What is there new, O my master?"

" The hakìm, that excellent man, assures me that my daughter cannot live."

Zeyd laughed, a short and angry laugh. " Is he then Allah ? " he asked scornfully.

But Shems-ud-dìn no longer heard him.

CHAPTER XIII

"THY son—since the first day he has not visited thee. Allah guard me from begetting one like him."

The reproach of Zeyd, scarce heeded at the moment, linked Shems-ud-dìn's reveries on the morrow of its utterance, recurring often like a sad refrain. It prevented his submersion in that stupor of prayerful musing which was his comfort. Yet not until noon was past, and the shadow of the gracious dome drew out to eastward, did it hold the foreground of his thought.

The aged Mahmûd Ali had come to sit with him awhile, and was reciting words of comfort in the high mosque voice, when Shems-ud-dìn asked himself, Was Abd-ur-Rahman all to blame? Had not the father likewise a duty toward the son? To be sure that his mind did not err, he said presently to the aged sheykh, his comforter:

"O my brother, hear a case and pronounce on it. A certain man had offspring a son and daughter, those two only, both dear to him. Yet did the balance of his love incline toward the daughter. One day he appeared to slight the boy, making much of the girl. And the boy was angry and drew away from him. Was the right with the son or the father? Upon which of them two rests the obligation?"

Zeyd, the son of Abbâs, on his heels out in the sunlight, emitted an "Ah!" of breathless interest. The aged Mahmûd Ali stroked his beard, reflecting. At length he replied:

"There is right with both of them, and against both. But the higher right is with the son. For did not his father reverse the ordinance of God by setting the woman above the man? Less is expected from a woman, it is for that she should receive less. I perceive that the case is thine. Is the son with thee in this city?"

"Let the case be a case like another," said Shems-ud-dìn, unwilling to betray his son's name.

Zeyd moaned. "It is too much for me. My blessedness is become a pain in my side. Surely never till now was man, poor and ignorant like me, privileged to hear such wisdom."

The verdict of the Chief of the Learned removed all hesitation from the mind of Shems-ud-dìn. Accordingly, about the fourth hour after noon, some time before he was wont to repair to the side of Alia, he entered the streets of the city, and bade Zeyd discover the whereabouts of the Bey's lodging. In this they experienced no difficulty, everyone consulted making haste to direct them with reverence for the callers on so great a man. Zeyd, finding his beggarly appearance overlooked, grew less rigid in dislike of a youth whose name had so genial an influence. Still it was with relief, on arrival at their destination, that he heard the doorkeeper inform his master that the Bey was out, and unlikely to return ere night.

The tidings cast down Shems-ud-dìn. Made aimless by disappointment, he wandered in the streets. Zeyd followed unobtrusively, his shadow always. The disciple was racking his brain for an array of words fine and imposing enough to comfort one so accomplished, when, in passing the entrance of a tavern, Shems-ud-dìn happened to glance therein.

"Praise to Allah!" he exclaimed suddenly. "Behold him there. He is found." And he turned in beneath the low arch, Zeyd at his heels.

The vault within struck dark and very cool. It was empty save for the proprietor (a portly Nazarene) and a group of three Turkish officers set on stools round a small table. Of these, two seemed sons of an Arab; but the fez of the third and eldest sealed the face of a Frank. The eyes of this last were blue, his cheeks ruddy, his mustache had the color of ripe wheat.

At Shems-ud-dìn's glad cry the three turned startled faces. Only one rose up in response to his salutation, and that was Abd-ur-Rahman. The other two kept their seats, staring aghast at the intrusion. And Abd-ur-Rahman did not rush to embrace his father, but hung back, the picture of irresolution.

Blind to this reluctance, Shems-ud-dìn took a stool beside his son, while Zeyd crossed his legs upon the ground hard by.

"I come to reproach thee a little, O my dear! Why hast thou failed my soul these many days when I need thy love for a staff? Thou hast shown no concern for Alia, who often cries for thee. It is not kind, O beloved!"

"O my eyes, I have so much business. Ask of these, my companions, and they will certify thee."

"Ah, by Allah, business enough to kill ten yoke of oxen, yet we survive somehow," affirmed he of the red face mockingly. "Drink something, old man. With me the money."

"May thy wealth increase; I am not thirsty," said Shems-ud-dìn stiffly, disliking the man's tone. "What is that thou drinkest, O my son? It must be precious as attar of roses to be served in so small a glass. Doubtless it is some sherbet new to me. The caterers invent fresh kinds from year to year."

Abd-ur-Rahman muttered unintelligibly. He had done all man could to conceal his glass.

"That is it, by Allah," laughed the two others. "A new sherbet. Taste and judge of its composition, O my uncle."

"I thank you, no." Shems-ud-dìn drew back from the glass thrust on him. He began to resent the manner of these youths. Why did not Abd-ur-Rahman restrain their insolence? He looked to his son in indignant appeal, but the lad's face was turned away, his attitude helpless.

"Then shall the valiant emìr, thy companion, taste thereof. Come, O Commander of the Faithful. Ennoble this little glass."

Zeyd, the son of Abbâs, took the glass held out to him, sniffed at the liquor, and then poured it out upon the ground.

"It is accursed, a sin for any man. Let the dirt drink it," he said coolly.

At that the jokers laughed immoderately.

"Thou dog!" cried he of the straw mustache, whose drink it was that was spilt. "Thou hast wasted a day's wage of one like thee. Thank Allah that I beat thee not until thou clog thy belly with the dirt it soaks."

But Abd-ur-Rahman joined not in their laughter. He kept his face averted from his father, and his whole pose announced such perfect wretchedness that Shems-ud-dìn, feeling concern for him, touched his arm, asking:

"What hurts thee, O my son?"

"Nothing. There is nothing," came the answer like a moan.

"It is this new sherbet," roared the other two. "It cools, and he has drunk too much of it. It has iced his belly. Fear not, O my uncle. He has a girl—ah, a beauty! who will expel the evil for him."

At that, perceiving they made game of him, the Sheykh Shems-ud-dìn arose with dignity.

"Allah shall teach you with punishment. Your own fathers are dishonored in that you respect not my beard and turban," he said; and without further words strode forth into the street, followed with alacrity by Zeyd, the son of Abbâs.

The tavern keeper, seeing customers driven forth before they had ordered anything, ran after and entreated them to remain and honor him. In low tones he apologized for the rudeness of the young officers.

"They have no manners, they respect nothing.

The others are bad enough, but that Nemsâwi is the lord of mischief. Before now he has broken my chattels without so much as a blessing. He pays for nothing. Keep it not against me, O my lords, but return and taste of something. Ennoble my poor place."

Shems-ud-dìn walked on, leaving him to groan and wring his hands upon the threshold.

The jeers of the young men accompanied the departure. But Abd-ur-Rahman neither spoke nor moved. The last Zeyd saw of him, his face was buried in his hands.

CHAPTER XIV

DEPRIVED of the counsel of Shems-ud-dîn, demoralized by confinement within walls, the little band of Circassians loitered in the markets with a sense of grievance. The sight of so many heathen —Franks and Nazarenes and unclean Jews—disgusted them in the city; and when they rode out to exercise their horses, the need to return went with them, killing pleasure, like the clank of a heavy chain.

At the end of ten days squandered in El Cûds, Hassan Agha was further from obtaining his rifles than he had been at first passing the gate. The soldiers avoided him; it seemed they had their orders. Abd-ur-Rahman, though smiling when they met in the street, steadfastly refused him audience. On the fourteenth day he faced the stern necessity, if they were to stay much longer in that money-eating place, of selling one of the lovely steeds which were their glory.

In a certain tavern he cast lots with his men, whose horse should go; and the lot fell upon Nesîb the

Thief, who straightway lifted up his voice and wept. Yet even he preferred the sacrifice to a shameful retreat, as though worsted by the boy Abd-ur-Rahman, while their beloved saint and his daughter, sole pretext of their coming, still abode in the city. They had taken it for granted beforehand that the cure of Alia by the wizard would be instantaneous, a mere wave of the hand, and resented its slowness as a deceit of the heathen dog.

Yet they were restrained from ventilating this grievance, and so easing their minds, by a captious whim of Hassan's to uphold the Frankish pig.

"He is an English physician. If Allah permits, he will perform his part," was the answer to their grumblings.

"What change is this, O lord Hassan!" cried one, thus repressed. "Is an Englishman other than a Frank, a vile infidel? Did they not deliver our land to the Muscovite, even while they touched our hands in friendship? How often hast thou denounced the whole brood of them?"

"Be silent!" Hassan commanded. "Taken separately they are good people—none better—brave and the slingstone of their word, but put together in the nation, they are treacherous as loose stones. Individuals of that race strove bravely with us against the Muscovite, while their nation betrayed them and us. It was commonly known in those days that this kind have neither honor nor nobility except when cut off. A strange people. Now this hakìm is cut off; he stands alone. Let be then, he will perform his covenant."

"In sh' Allah!" the band murmured, but this stopper on expression of their just annoyance only caused it to ferment.

In the temper to quarrel with their own shadows and kill whoever brushed against them, it was only by the courtesy or the cowardice of other wayfarers that they escaped embroilment. Even as it was, on two occasions their conduct called for the interference of the street watch.

In the wide open space before the tower, where fellahìn from Beyt-Laham and the surrounding villages stand to sell the produce of their fields, they one morning encountered Ismaìl, the doorkeeper of the Frank physician, going marketing, a basket on his arm.

Instantly Nesìb the Thief went mad, or so it seemed to his companions. Like a fierce dog, he flew snarling at the throat of the old negro.

"Pig! Whence hast thou that garment?"

"It is the gift of my master." The tall black

grinned as with a sweep of his long gnarled arm he flung off his assailant.

At that the fury of Nesìb passed all bounds. He drew the dagger from his waistband and sprang again, this time foaming at the mouth.

Again the strength of the negro felled him easily. But, seeing the old man's wrist bled from a scratch of the knife, Hassan Agha intervened. He dealt the Thief a cuff under the ear which sent him staggering up against a wall near by; and did the like for Ali, the bosom friend of the Thief, who had the rashness to cry shame on the blow.

By that time many people gathered toward them; and, spying soldiers, Shibli took to his heels.

"Cut his life! Burn his house! O Allah! O Lord!" raved Nesìb. "Is it not enough to lose my horse? The black pig wears my honor—O defilement! that princely garment. May his father perish! An heirloom in my family! Woe on us! I gave it to the Frank hakìm, and the black pig wears it. Oo—oo!"

The watch came and demanded to know the meaning of the disturbance. Hassan simply shrugged his shoulders and directed their gaze upon the maniac scrabbling at the wall. He said:

"It is a poor friend of mine who has had so many

and great misfortunes in a short time that, see, his mind is broken."

"The poor one. May Allah relieve him!" said the soldiers piously, and went their way. On their departure, Hassan gripped the Thief by the shoulders, and shook him till his tongue lolled out.

"Allah grant thy parents a shameful death! Be silent! What is this garment to lament—some mohair—a little braid?"

"It is an ancient garment—a most reverend garment—all my inheritance!" gasped the sufferer.

At that, past patience, Hassan seized his ears as they had been two handles, and, heedless of the shrieks of Ali, beat his head against the wall, saying:

"Speak no more of it! It was given from thee, not so? So the hakìm cure the daughter of Shems-ud-dìn, what matter who wears it? It has served its turn."

And Nesìb, dreading further punishment, fell silent, weeping upon Ali's breast.

Their second brawl was of a more public nature. It chanced, on an afternoon when the Nazarenes had a great ceremony in their church called the Resurrection, that Hassan and his men, attended as usual by Shibli, passed by the mouth of the bazaar leading down to the church, at an hour when the throng of worshipers poured forth. They were shouldering their way through that herd of infidels, when some men made resistance, pushing hard against them. Peering about him angrily, Hassan saw shawled heads and swarthy faces with eyes of smoldering fire.

"O happy day! May Allah destroy every Bedawi!" He spat in the face of the nearest.

In the twinkling of an eye there was a fray. Knives flashed, blood was drawn. Piercing screams of Frankish women came from the crowd around. The breath of each combatant was hot in the face of his antagonist, at such close quarters was the strife. One fell and was trampled under foot; another shrieked and threw up his hands, but was caught by a comrade.

All at once rang out a voice of command. The guard returning from the church had surrounded them in the nick of time. The struggle ceased magically. The soldiers, inured to such work, separated the two factions neatly without partiality or insult.

"It is a vengeance for blood," cried Hassan. "These dogs slew my two sons. They have paid no indemnity. My cause is just!"

"He is a liar; hear him not, O my lord! We know not him nor his sons."

"It is a blood feud; let them alone, O my children," said the officer in command of the detachment, a man advanced in years. "Drive the one party back toward the church, the other on toward the tower, that they be fairly sundered. . . . When thou, O old wolf, next requirest the price of blood, see thou choose some spot more seemly than the heart of the city. Is there not land enough open in all the world that thou must needs choose this place?"

"Art hurt, my son?" asked Hassan of Shibli, as they were driven toward the tower.

"Aye, and that sorely," replied the young man, nursing his two hands. "I had slain him who smote me, but that he escaped in the crowd."

"I smote thee, O valorous youth," laughed one at his side. "Thou didst clasp me so tight from behind that I was hampered, so I pricked thy two hands."

At that there was loud laughter, and Shibli hung his head.

"That soldier spoke sense," observed Hassan later, when, freed from surveillance, they were returning to the khan. "Outside the walls is best for battle as for everything else. Thy horse is preserved to thee, O Thief. To-morrow, or the day after, we retire from the city. It is good at least to know that those Bedû are not favored above us. They have not procured rifles, or would they still be here among the jumpers of walls? By Allah's leave, we may chance on their camping ground and make an end. At least, if Allah will, we can glean a little, out of sight of the garrison."

"We shall have all the wealth of the land, I swear it, so only that I keep my horse," cried the Thief in rapture.

It was with enthusiasm that all to whom Hassan spoke on the morrow heard of his decision to quit the city. His open abuse of a government which could refuse a few rifles to men worn out in its service, had alarmed the timorous and supple townsmen. He had inveighed against Abd-ur-Rahman Bey, a young man of the first influence, in terms almost treasonable, calling him selfish and impious, a dog who pushed back the gift of an old friend, and was above speaking to his own father. Sober men frown on such talk, and a certain rich merchant, overhearing some of it, had observed:

"These men are possessed with blind devils. Is it to be supposed that Abd-ur-Rahman will show them kindness when they defame him in the markets? And can he now let them take the rifles? I will give you my neighbor's hoard privately, as between ourselves; but blab the matter beforehand, and I avert my face,

I draw my robe away, I have no knowledge of you. As for what the old braggart says about Abd-ur-Rahman's father, it is a lie. Abd-ur-Rahman is an orphan, both of father and mother. I have the assurance of it from his own mouth."

That merchant, with the other tavern haunters, was aware how often men who hear sedition and rebuke not its prophet, are themselves made guilty of it in the eye of Power. And Hassan, in the midst of his adherents, looked ill to rebuke. The coffee sellers, therefore, joined with their customers in extolling the wisdom of his plan to depart. They praised his intelligence, and that of his honorable companions. The city was no place for them. It was a malicious place, a backbiting and slanderous place, the home of all injustice. No wonder their Excellencies preferred the open land; and so on.

Hassan, the dupe of these plaudits, was returning in great satisfaction from his morning round, when he saw from a distance a man beckoning to him beside the doorway of the khan. Drawing near, he recognized the Bimbashi Muhammed. "Ma sh' Allah!" he exclaimed in his soul; for he had thought never again to behold that particular rascal.

"Deign to step apart with me," said the soldier, with lowly reverence; and, when Hassan had complied, he touched his uniform piteously, calling attention to a change in it. "See, I have been degraded. I have suffered much for thy sake. Thou wilt not give up the undertaking, surely—thou, a great one—for the fee is like owing to me for all I have endured. I come to tell thee that vigilance is relaxed, that all is now favorable to our business—but to learn from the lord of the khan that your honors depart in the morning. Go not far away, O my dear! Return by night to the city. I will warn the guards at the city gate; I myself will admit thee to the tower. I cannot bring you the things because of a sacred oath which was wrung from me. But I can open the door of the armory. Fear not, O my master. There is no danger, Allah witness. At the fourth hour of the night. And the fee—we agreed upon that. Forget not the fee, O my eyes, for I have suffered much."

Once more he touched his mutilated uniform in the manner of a beggar showing sores. Hassan pulled his white mustache, and eyed the man grimly askance.

"It is not good to deceive Hassan Agha."

The poor soldier flung up his hands. "Allah witness," he cried, in tones of real horror. "O my great lord, trust Muhammed. I am a poor honest man whose one aim is to serve thee and obtain the reward."

"Agreed then," said Hassan, well content. "To-morrow, at the fourth hour of the night, be ready. With my peace, go."

Muhammed blessed him and went. His tone throughout, though cringing, had been straightforward, without a trace of that conscious subtlety which had disfigured his behavior upon former occasions. It was the manner of a merchant who, seeing his customer in act to depart, through fear of losing him, speaks truth for the first time.

CHAPTER XV

It was close upon sunrise when Hassan Agha and his men threaded the burrows of the city to the northern gate. Few moved abroad beside themselves. Dogs slunk drowsily along by the walls, seeking lairs for the day. Once past the gate and its stretching shadow, they all with one accord clapped spurs to their horses.

Away they galloped, shouting, through olive groves where the sunrise reddened one side of the knotty trunks, and awoke a pearly sheen in the gray mistlike foliage. Past old rock tombs, past caverns fledged with fern, they dashed in the pink of morning. From an eminence, the city walls appeared a blue cloud line just beneath the sun. The rays smote their shoulders with a loving hand. They were free.

Shibli rode with them by indulgence of the Sheykh Shems-ud-dìn, before whom they had laid their plan overnight. The saint had heard them listlessly, as from a distance. He had approved of everything with the slight impatience of one in haste to be rid of questions. But not so Zeyd, the son of Abbâs. Sure that they were bent on some iniquity, the fellâh had done all in the power of grimaces and private signals to arouse misgiving in his master, all in vain; till at length, with a shrug for an obtuseness which he knew for the God-sent rind of sanctity, he accepted the inevitable. Executing a circular bow to comprise all the enemy, he had besought them to brighten once again the village of his wife's sister's husband's uncle, who, poor good man, would thus be rendered the happiest of living creatures. When Hassan welcomed the suggestion, Zeyd had praised Allah as for a favor done to himself. He looked to harvest from the lips of his distant relative such clear evidence of their wickedness as should convince even a saint's incredulity.

But Hassan was not going to seek that village until the evening. He wished to celebrate the release from entombing walls by a day's ride in quest of adventure.

Letting the horses resume a quiet pace, they joked and chatted together, while the land led them onward by waves. At length, from between some ancient olive trees which watched a sea of corn, they beheld a flat-roofed village with three upper chambers like towers projecting above the herd of dwellings.

"There, in sh' Allah, we will break our fast,"

said Hassan, to the joy of Shibli, who, from excessive delight in the ride, was very hungry.

At the foot of a little height the village crowned, were women fetching water from the spring. Their pitchers filled, they stood to gossip, with arms akimbo. On beholding a crowd of riders, they huddled together in alarm. Other women, at work in the field hard by, stood up to stare at the strangers. A man with a preposterous turban came forth from the village, yawning, with arms upraised. He had begun to descend toward the spring, when he, too, caught sight of the horsemen, and stood still beneath a young fig tree, his hand shading his eyes.

"We be soldiers," shouted Hassan, loud enough to be heard of the man in the distance. "O women, conduct us to the house of your sheykh."

At that the women raised a wail, and wrung their hands. The man by the fig tree ran back whence he came.

"O Allah, have mercy. What have our men worth requiring? O my lords, there is nothing left with us. All our beasts are dead lately of a murrain. A blight is on our crops these many years."

"Draw near, O rising moon," said Hassan, ogling the youngest and most lissome of the group. "Fear not, O delight. It is but a drink from thy pitcher. O mothers of mighty men, give to drink to my companions. We are not wild beasts to devour you. Why so afraid?"

A moment they hung in a flutter. Then the girl, enticed of Hassan, took a bold step forward, giggling at her companions. She held up her pitcher. Having drunk his fill, Hassan hugged her in his arms. She gave but a little scream and struggled faintly, giggling. Louder screams and laughter came from the elder women, caught in like manner. The toilers in the field applauded the pretty game.

"By Allah, my old mouth waters. My soul is sick for desire of thee," said Hassan, with the pant of love. "For the sake of all you women—how beautiful! how seductive!—we will spare this village. Say I not well, O my children? We will ask no more of the sheykh than to make for us a little feast to confirm friendship. My peace on you."

At that the girl who had served Hassan set off, running with rhythmic hips, the pitcher poised upon her head. Before the horsemen reached the house of the sheykh, she had convoked all the men of the place to do them honor. Impressed by her breathless, eager tale, those villagers were ready to make a holiday, to roast a sheep, and gorge thereon till night, to spit a dozen fowls, to boil a hill of rice. But Hassan magnanimously bade them spare their pains. He asked only bread and curds, a few olives, a cup of coffee, for himself and each of his following. The crowd lost speech in wonder at his moderation. His frugal needs were at once supplied.

When he and all his company were satisfied, the villagers led them forth with praise upon their way. At the foot of a rocky slope they said farewell.

"What is the name of yonder shrine?" asked Hassan, pointing with his hand to a mountain, on the summit of which, up against the sky, appeared the form of a wely or saint's tomb.

"His name is Neby Samwìl, may it please your Excellency," the reply was given by a score of voices.

"Is it a great shrine?"

The villagers shrugged shoulders, and smiled widely, glancing at one another. It was as his Excellency pleased. Some pilgrims went there.

The cavalcade rode on by rough and stony ways, while the sun on their backs shone hot and hotter. Wild flowers grew in beds between the rocks. Now and then a bird cried. The hues of earth in contrast with the deep blue sky were pale and dead, as sands beside the sea. A train of camels, pursuing some other road, appeared and disappeared, mere dots upon the sky line.

Coming in sight of another village, hardly separate from its surrounding rocks, Hassan called the Thief to his side and gave some orders, heard of Shibli, who rode near. "Take one other with thee," were the concluding words.

"Let me be that one," pleaded Shibli eagerly.

"Thou, the scholar, the disciple of the Sheykh Shems-ud-dìn. Allah forbid!"

"Nay, let me. I would show you all that I am not a coward. And in truth, since the girl Alia is in the way of recovery, I care not what becomes of me."

"Go, then," said Hassan, between a grin and a sneer. "And see that thou support our Thief properly, else Ali, his friend, will surely beat thee."

Shibli dropped behind with Nesìb, while Hassan and the rest of the party rode on in earnest conference.

At entering the village, Ali, the only Arab left to them, cried aloud by Hassan's orders, so that all who rested from the heat looked forth at their doors:

"O good people, O pious Muslimûm, come out and see. Lo! here be pilgrims of distinction—holy men, none like them—men of renown. They come from Jebel Câf, that mountain reaching into heaven, which is the boundary of the whole earth. From

Jebel Câf, I say, to visit your Neby Samwìl, the illustrious, the blessed. It is an honor done to all your land. Come forth and behold that which no poor man ever yet was privileged to see—princes from Jebel Câf, which is under heaven."

And when all the inhabitants stood gaping in their doorways:

"Come forth," he cried, "beyond the houses. Let all see and hear alike. This place is too narrow."

Then, having lured them out into the open, Ali there addressed them at great length; bidding them be good ever more, and sin never again, for that they were now ennobled above all their fathers, having beheld the kings of Jebel Câf, the very Gate of Heaven, who come once in a thousand years. Their crops would increase thenceforth; all provisions in their houses would abound miraculously. In the end, he besought Hassan to bless them, and then rode off, leaving them perfectly bewildered.

Scarcely were they out of sight of those simpletons, when they espied Shibli and the Thief seated under a rock beside the path, holding their steeds by the headropes.

"It was the work of a minute," cried Shibli, much excited. "We have many useful things, but alas! no money. Nesìb has ten fowls which he caught and bagged before I could have laid hand on one of them. Also, he changed some things from house to house, so that those fellahìn may suspect one another of the theft. He is a devil, this Thief. I had been naught without him."

Hassan looked hard at the speaker. "The praise to Allah," he said, "we have now two thieves instead of one."

The boy's eyes flashed with anger, and his lips parted to make answer. The next minute his eyes swam in tears, and he hung his head, silenced. For long he spoke no word to anyone, but rode apart in dudgeon or despondency.

They came to a wady trending eastward athwart their road. A fairly defined goat path ran along its hither bank. Saying they had gone far enough in a straight line from the city, Hassan led the way upon that narrow track, the rest following him in single file.

They had not proceeded far in the new direction ere their leader reined up. The track was gone. But the sharp eyes of Nesìb made out a village in the distance where they could be sure of learning the way. Hassan resigned the post of leader to the Thief, himself riding second in the file. He could thus converse with Nesìb without fear of being overheard.

"We have no money," he said savagely. "Look

to it that we obtain some before evening. How can we enter the Tower, how fee the soldiers, without money? I myself will help thee, if thou fearest a bold stroke."

"No money." Nesìb's shoulders went up to his ears on the shrug of despair. "I will do what is possible, O my dear lord! But money is not like fowls, nor yet like flowers by the wayside. Allah witness, I can neither catch nor pluck it. I know not beforehand where it lies. It must come to my hand, or I cannot take it. Allah put it near me, since our need is urgent."

At the entering in of the village Nesìb had spied from afar, grew a fine tree, beneath which, at the hour of their approach, lay two sturdy youths asleep. These being awakened, one of them gladly undertook to guide their honors to a place whence the road ran clear to El Cûds. For half an hour he led them in and out among the stony hills till, near a village superior in size and structure to any they had yet seen, he set them on a wide track and pointed out their direction. Receiving some small coins for his services, he cried on Allah to increase their wealth.

"May Allah heed him," muttered Hassan, "for he has our last dinâr."

The sun was still high when they learnt from

some other wayfarers that they were again near to the city and within a short hour of the village of Zeyd's relation. Hassan bade Shibli and the rest go on thither, while he and Nesìb attended to some business they had to transact in common. With laughter and knowing looks, the troop rode off.

Hassan and the Thief urged their horses up a small, steep hill, from the top of which they beheld the city, and much country on all hands. Beneath them in the dale they had just left were many olive trees a-shimmer in the sun, which cast a filigree of shade upon the field and on the bridle path which wound among them. Having secured their horses out of sight, they sat to watch that path.

At last, when from long watching he had dropped to sleep, old Hassan was aroused by an exclamation from the Thief at his side. He presently became aware of figures moving upon the path, drawing near out of the distance.

He perceived a fat man bestriding a tall black jackass, and beside him a servant, walking, holding a sunshade over the fat one's head. The donkey bore full saddlebags, to judge from the angle of projection of his rider's legs. And the fat man kept clutching the bosom of his robe, as if that, too, were not empty.

"Come, O my lord. Let us descend," hissed Nesìb. "Yon old man has our money. Watch his hands; observe his glance of fear to every side. Y'Allah!"

They stole rapidly down the hill, making use of every scrap of cover. Long before the fat man and his servant reached the place of their descent, two simple men, an old and a young, sat by the roadside, beneath a wall that fenced the olive yards, holding one another's hand, enjoying innocent converse in that shady spot. The younger of the twain crooned a love song with closed eyes.

All at once, as the black donkey came ambling by, the pair sprang up suddenly, while the elder presented a large and very curious pistol at the rider's head.

Upon that, seeing the miscreants were two, himself but one, the servant turned and fled with the open sunshade. A minute later, when the fat man lay on the ground, puffing and cursing beneath the clever hands of Nesìb, Hassan saw that servant afar off, frantically endeavoring to climb a tree, while the parasol, still open, adorned the ground close by, seeming some strange white flower.

At that instant Nesìb swore roundly. The fat man had bitten deep into the wrist of his despoiler.

"Pig of a citizen!" yelled the Thief. "I will tear thy beard out. I will stab thy filthy eyes."

He kicked his victim, and would have leapt upon the hill of fatness had not Hassan Agha restrained him.

"Nevertheless, he shall be punished, and that at once," said the Circassian. "We asked but his wealth; Allah witness, we bore no grudge to this man more than to any other. But now, since he curses me and has bitten my companion, the case is altered."

So saying, he removed the saddlebags from the donkey's back, then, letting go the bridle, drove his dagger into its flank. The black jackass screamed, plunged, and careered away.

Nesìb, meanwhile, was employed in tearing the raiment off the fallen fat one, now quite paralyzed with rage. The despoiled gasped and gurgled convulsively.

"O Allah, help! Shall men rob and outrage the Câdi of El Cûds, within call of the city, and live? May Allah burn the abode of your wickedness. By Allah, I shall be revenged. The day will come when I shall send you forth to death. All robbers return to me. I am the Câdi."

"Câdi or pig, thou hadst no right to bite my hand," replied Nesìb severely.

Having stripped him to his silken shirt and his voluminous drawers of white calico, Nesìb, for a further insult, hoodwinked him with his own turban, and bound together his wrists and ankles with strips cut from the clothing taken from him. Then after Hassan he climbed back over the wall.

From a discreet place they watched what should befall. They saw the servant clamber down from out his tree of refuge and, hesitating, with fearful glances, approach his master. They saw him fumble with the bonds. They heard the fat man's scream of rage, when at length he could rise; and observed him spit upon that servant, striking his face repeatedly, so that the coward fell on his knees and howled for mercy. They waited to see no more, but, full of quiet mirth, crept on their way.

CHAPTER XVI

When Hassan Agha and the Thief reached the abode of Zeyd's wife's relation, the sun had just sunk beneath the western hill. The cooling waters of the twilight overflowed the village and all the wady. They found their comrades at the sheykh's house instated in the best room, the floor of which was laid for a feast. The entire population crowded round the open door, anxious to observe the manners of guests so honorable.

"Allah witness, we will be no burden on you," said Hassan to their entertainer, after fervent greetings. "We have money and, moreover, we shall count it an honor to espouse your quarrels. Your friends, our friends; your foes, our foes; your people are from this hour the sworn brothers of my people."

"May Allah reward your Excellencies! Behold, we are dirt. The honor is too great!" The old fellâh wagged his turbaned head most humbly.

"I with four of my comrades repair to the city this night; but after a little while we shall return. In the meanwhile, here is a trifle. Honor me by accepting. It is only right, since we are so great a company."

The sheykh of the village looked with awful reverence upon a piece of shining gold. It seemed he dared not take it. But when Hassan thrust it into his palm, his fist clinched on it instantly. He faltered praise to God, then wept a little.

About the third hour of night, Hassan set out once more, taking with him Shibli and four of his own men, the Thief among them. Once past the city gate, it was his intention to send Shibli straight to the khan. He had no wish to earn the rebuke of Shems-ud-dìn by involving the youth in any serious mischief. But as they rode along, Shibli pleaded so earnestly to be allowed this opportunity of conquering his native cowardice, that Hassan, foreseeing no danger, had not the heart to deny him. After all, they were bound on no adventure, but a simple business of fetching and carrying, which could hurt no one.

In an olive grove at no great distance from the walls, they dismounted and made fast the steeds, leaving one of their number in charge of them. They had not taken many steps from that place, the ground being most uneven, when, with a yell, a man suddenly disappeared below the surface of the earth. Eying one another in terror, they missed the Thief.

A groan came from near at hand, ushering words of anguish.

"Woe on me! Am I not most wretched? Do not all things conspire against me? A black hog wears my robe of honor; the lot falls on me to lose my horse; a fat man bites my wrist in two; and now the earth has opened his mouth and devoured me. Allah, mercy! Woe! Woe on us!"

The Thief had stepped into a cistern long disused. Leaning on their bellies round the brink, they managed to grip hold of him, and at length, heaving together, brought him up to the surface. He sank upon the earth with a cry of pain. His legs were broken, he asserted again and again. Useless for the expedition, he was ordered to crawl back and keep watch over the horses, while the man before charged with that duty took on active service.

It was dark on all the face of the land. The city wall was but a greater darkness as they followed it on to the gate. Here they passed unchallenged. The men in the guardhouse peeped out, laughing, and wished them a happy night.

The bulk of the ancient fortress rose undefined against the sky, which in that quarter showed no stars. Clouds seemed to be rising, it might be for a thunderstorm, the year's last rain. On the narrow bridge which crossed the trench to the portal, Hassan whispered:

"O Muhammed!"

"Ready, O my lord," came the answer aloud.

"Is all well?"

"Be sure it is. No need to whisper. Only friends hear us."

"Then open and show us the place."

"Gently, gently, O Excellency! I would first hold thy gift in my hand, for an earnest of good faith. Be not angry with Muhammed. Bethink thee, I know thee but a little. And I have grave need of the money. To thee it is nothing; to me much. Deign to indulge thy servant, O my soul!"

"Good. Then I give thee the half. The other half shall be thine when we come out with the things."

"At thy pleasure, O lord of bounty!"

The gate was then opened, and Hassan made his gift to the sentry. Muhammed peered at the money and turned it over slowly, seeming dissatisfied. Weighing it in his hand, he remonstrated:

"O my eyes, this is very little. For me alone, it might suffice. But there are many besides me your helpers in this business. Think not I could act as I do, without the connivance of one or two of my superiors. Then . . . the guard at the gate. . . ."

" See here, take this and be content." Hassan doubled the sum given.

" It will serve, perhaps," said Muhammed, with a shrug. " Come, follow me." But he continued to grumble in an undertone.

Though the gate was left ostentatiously open behind them, Shibli felt imprisoned. Too late, he repented of his rashness in aspiring to vie with brave men. As they followed the soldier across the yard, he kept close to Hassan Agha for protection.

Their guide unlocked a heavy door. He struck a match and, shielding the flame with his hand, showed them steps leading down to a vault.

" Deign to enter. Ennoble these Frankish matches."

" May thy house be destroyed! We need more light than those provide," objected Hassan testily.

" Cut thy life! " retorted Muhammed in anger. " Didst think I would carry a lantern hither through the common yard, to show any man our business who may happen to be awake and looking out? By Allah, you expect much, and give mighty little! "

" Aha, is it the smallness of the gift, my brother? Thou shalt have more, much more, when we come forth with the rifles."

Mollified by this assurance, Muhammed said more civilly:

"On the right, a few paces from the foot of the stair, you will find a lantern hanging by the wall. Be careful to strike no match in the armory itself, for there is much gunpowder."

"Shibli, stay without and watch," ordered Hassan.

"No, no! Let me enter. For the love of Allah, let me enter with you," cried the youth, panic-stricken at the prospect of being left alone.

"No, it were a sin for thee."

"Enter none the less," whispered Muhammed. "It is a dungeon worth seeing. The walls, the roofs, the pillars, are of the rarest workmanship. I will keep watch instead of thee."

Shibli required no urging to fulfill his one desire. He slipped in after the Circassians, and the soldier, as if for a precaution, closed the door behind him.

He felt his way down eight stone steps till he found hard-trodden earth beneath his feet.

Presently, amid the darkness ahead of him, there broke a storm of curses. A match was struck, forming a cocoon of light in the distance. Hassan cried in a terrible voice:

"Here is no lantern—no armory. And the door

is shut upon us. We are trapped, entombed. May Allah slay me where I stand if I slay not ten men for this trick upon us."

Shibli crouched at the foot of the steps, annihilated, a drumming in his ears. All at once the door above opened, and shrouded figures entered from the lesser darkness. It shut again ere Hassan and the rest could come at it.

Shibli trembled as those forms brushed by him. The smell of them was not the smell of men, but of goats or camels, he knew not which. A guttural oath from one of them and the words, " I touch a man," uttered in a tone of alarm, failed to humanize them. But the stroke of a match and a gladsome shout from Hassan—" The Bedû! Thanks to Allah!"—relieved him of the shudder of the unknown, while multiplying his fears a hundredfold. For that shout was prelude to a frightful conflict of men fighting tooth and nail in the dark, panting hard in the death grapple, striking what they could not see.

Shibli heard groans, gasps, short screams of rage, and the struggling fall of heavy bodies. His heart beat in his brain. He shrank back up the steps to the very door.

Just then the door opened, and, like a sword flash, out leapt the maddened youth. He broke through two ranks of soldiers, oversetting some of them. He was endued with the strength of ten men by the mortal fright possessing him. Blinded by the shine of many lanterns, he missed the gate at first and struck the wall beside it. Rebounding and quickly collecting himself, he dashed for the startled sentry, who, concluding he had to deal with a supernatural agent, wisely dodged the encounter.

"One has escaped, O my lord," reported the soldier Muhammed to his captain. "A youth, but a youth of the devils. As well try to catch a bullet."

"What matter! . . . Have you stopped the fight in there? Drive them all forth."

Hassan Agha and his three comrades, with all who remained of their antagonists, emerged, torn and bleeding, from the cellar. They blinked in the glare of the lanterns. To their dazed apprehension it seemed the whole city was arrayed against them. By degrees their senses cleared somewhat. Having dashed the blood from his eyes, Hassan descried Abd-ur-Rahman.

"Ma sh' Allah! Thou here, O child of my soul? Is it a trick of thine? By my gun, thou hast fooled us perfectly. It was a stratagem worthy of thy father's brother, worthy of Milhem Basha, the very parent of guile."

In the same playful tone Abd-ur-Rahman answered:

" It seemed desirable to read thee a little lesson, O beloved. Thy endeavor has been to defame me; thou madest light of my commands. To-night thou hast thy wages."

" But as for thee, I will pay thee soon or late, thou lying dog." Hassan turned fiercely upon the soldier Muhammed.

That deceiver only laughed. " I scoff at thee, old dotard. Thou art cross, it is natural. What is that to me? I am once more Bimbashi, which is all I care about. If thou didst think to outwit our young lord here—thou with but two old eyes and the mind of a bull—well, Allah bless thee, that is all."

" What care I? " said Hassan, assuming a jaunty air. " I have at least done something to pay off a debt of long standing. We have slain a few of these dwellers in the House of Hair, who slew my two sons. To Allah praise therefore."

" Now Allah witness. We knew thee not, nor had ground of quarrel with thee," cried a Bedawi, who stood by, very sadly. " But now you have slain my father and my brother, their blood cries for your blood. It may prove a long story, but the end is already written."

A snarl of thunder in the distance gave a sinister voice to the darkness which encompassed the lighted crowd. Hassan Agha turned again to Abd-ur-Rahman.

"What would a certain old man think of this treatment of one who loved thee?" he asked with deep meaning, almost with authority. "What would the saintly——"

"Enough said!" cried Abd-ur-Rahman; and by the haste of his ejaculation Hassan knew himself secure from public dishonor. "I intend not to disgrace so old a friend. Pay ten pounds Turk for distribution among the soldiers under my command, or in default of that sum—which I think you could hardly make up among you—give me a mare from your cavalry, and it is finished between us."

"The money is with me," said Hassan, with a chastened gleam of satisfaction; for he knew that Abd-ur-Rahman desired the mare. A gleeful murmur spread among the soldiery.

"With these sons of wandering I will be lenient in like manner. Ten pounds Turk, or one of their thoroughbred mares; that is the price of escape. But first, in their case, it is necessary that I see some certificate of their discharge from the military service."

"A'al! He is wise. May Allah preserve Abd-ur-Rahman, coming glory of the realm."

Hassan stayed to hear no more. He paid his fine with the money taken from the Câdi, and slunk away out of the sphere of the lantern light. Hearing laughter, he ground his teeth and vowed vengeance senselessly. The watch at the gate of the city turned out to mock him and his companions, inquiring whence those blood stains, where the rifles, and so forth.

Flashes of lightning illumined the country fitfully. The stars were covered. Thunder rolled, now near, now distant. In the olive grove where they had left their steeds, it began to rain, big drops, which shook the leaves. The whinny and stamp of the horses guiding them, they found the place.

The Thief lay on his back, groaning, just as they had left him. His legs were broken, he moaned. He told how, as he lay looking up at the sky, he had seen a sword flash forth from heaven over the Holy City, and heard a great voice cry:

"Die, all of you!"

He supposed that Allah would destroy those wicked townsfolk, and Hassan thought it very likely.

CHAPTER XVII

"GREAT has been my sin. I will hide none of it from thee. The face of the girl struck terror in me when I beheld it that time beneath the magic tree. My soul abhorred her. I prayed—O my more than father, curse me not! I prayed that thy child might die. And when thy worthier prayers prevailed, when she came safe to the Frank physician, I cared not what thing I became. I gave up my soul to wickedness; I exchanged thy wise company for that of the noisy ones; I entered into every device of Hassan Agha and his companions; I surpassed them all in violence; I robbed, I fought, I slew. Last night I slew Allah knows how many men. I alone was granted strength to escape that I might ask thy forgiveness. All the rest, the fierce, the mighty ones, are dead."

Shibli, who had stood beating his breast before Shems-ud-dìn, here fell down upon the ground and wept convulsively.

With the sun he had come to the Haràm, to the cell where, from distress of mind, the sheykh had chosen to pass that night of storm. Shems-ud-dìn knew not what to make of his mad appearance and wild words. The bondman of far other griefs, he looked at Zeyd, then at surrounding objects—the fair Dome set as a rock in mid-stream of the sunrise, some dark forms crowned with white turbans stalking gravely in its shadow—but could only shake his head and smile wearily. He saw no sense anywhere. The soft, husky coo of pigeons, the golden calm, discredited that tale of sin and horror.

"May Allah take my life also," moaned Shibli, prostrate on the time-worn pavement. "I am unworthy to live longer in thy sight. As I lay all night in the door of the khan, supposing thee to be within, the wrath of Allah thundered against me. I cannot survive this hour."

The sheykh glanced at Zeyd with raised eyebrows, as who should say, What make you of this riddle? The fellâh replied:

"He is distraught. Be sure it is some bad joke of the sons of Eblìs. By some contrivance they have driven him mad with fear. May Allah affright the whole race of them, and that suddenly."

"Alas, wish no evil upon them, for they are dead. All of them slain in the darkness under ground. I alone broke away."

Shems-ud-dìn gazed with compassion upon the sobbing liar. His mind, purged by grief, saw round the story and accurately appraised it.

"Do a kindness, O Zeyd," he said at length. "Go to the Chief of the Learned. At this hour thou wilt find him in the mosque El Aksa. Repeat to him the tale, and beseech him to ascertain the truth for us. He has influence with the rulers of the city, and can come at the rights of it."

Zeyd sped on the errand. Shibli lay crushed before the sheykh, groaning and weeping, praying for death and forgiveness.

"What can I do to atone? O lord, I will marry thy daughter when the Frank has healed her. See, my soul is between thy two feet."

In accents of mild wonder the sheykh replied:

"What is this thou sayest of my daughter? Allah forbid that I should victimize thee. Never, unless by the especial grace of Allah, will she live to be given in marriage. Why hast thou hid thy thought from me? I had not blamed nor in any wise constrained thee. The affections of a young man are winds blowing hot or cold on him; he discerns neither their goal nor their origin; nor can in aught control them. He can but entreat Allah to order them for his soul's weal. Is it for this thou hast shunned me these many days? Be comforted. I forgive thee, O my son."

The convulsion of Shibli's frame abated gradually till he lay in peace, broken only at lengthening intervals by a kind of catch in the breath, like a hiccough. The coo of the mosque pigeons again predominated.

Zeyd soon returned, accompanied by a tall black-bearded man of somber habit, with eyes of coal set deep in a sallow visage.

"The revered Mahmûd in this hour vouchsafes instruction to his disciples. He cannot himself come to thee. But with his peace, and in hope of thy forgiveness, he sends an excellent sheykh who can certify thee concerning the whole matter, being already apprised of it from the mouth of his brother, a high officer of the garrison."

Zeyd delivered the message with unction. The words of the Chief of the Learned were as sweetmeats in his mouth.

With a formal salutation the reverend sheykh, thus presented, sat down crosslegged before the cell, and spoke as follows:

"Know, O my uncle, that there exists among the garrison of this city a youth of good lineage and high influence, his name Abd-ur-Rahman Bey. The same, coming lately in charge of the armory, forbade those thefts of rifles and ammunition, by connivance of the soldiery, which are common in provincial garrisons. But his subordinates, accustomed to view official prohibitions but as pretty cloaks, proceeded, at the time of the great feast of the Nazarenes, when all kinds of people flock to our city, to negotiate as usual for the sale of rifles. Abd-ur-Rahman has an eagle's eyesight. He discovered their disobedience, and punished it severely, degrading some of the culprits, imprisoning others. Then, hearing how those who had hoped to obtain arms, proclaimed in the taverns their intention still to get them in his despite, he set a trap for the boasters. He sent out those soldiers whom he had before punished, to entice them to the Tower, securing fidelity in his agents by the promise of his favor should they succeed.

"Allah prospered his strategy. Last night a great number of Circassians and a whole tribe of the Bedû were trapped by him in a dungeon beneath the Tower; where, in the dark, the two nations fell to fighting to such purpose that, when the door was opened, only four of either faction were left alive." ("The praise to Allah," interjected Shibli. "All four of them lived to emerge.") "Then Abd-ur-Rahman, seeing they had punished one another, grew lenient. He laid a fine upon each party. The

Circassians paid the fine and went free. The Bedû, lacking money, offered instead a fine mare of the best blood of the desert. But Abd-ur-Rahman, having chanced to find out that none of them had served his time in the army, holds them prisoners, and has taken all their horses. That is the whole story, O my uncle."

"How plain I see thee, O my brother Milhem," murmured Shems-ud-dìn, with a deep sigh. "O Allah, behold the wickedness done in this city which Thou hast hallowed."

"Ah, there I hold with thee, O my uncle," said the black-bearded sheykh heartily. "She is indeed the mistress of perversity, this city, whose soil is holy. The like has been observed of El Khalìl and other sanctuaries, and especially of Mekka itself. The wicked throng the markets of the good. It is lucky that we of the congregation can still exert some sway over the agents of government, or El Cûds would be polluted and defiled by those who, if their faith were earnest, should esteem her most highly—that is, by the Nazarenes. Not once or twice have we opposed the establishment of a place of ribaldry by certain Franks, who still importune the authorities. And we allow no harlot within our gates. The Council of Notables sides with us, fortunately, or the town would soon be as foul with naked sin as are the cities of the Franks. The government would soon succumb to the temptation of their bribes. . . ."

The young sheykh, whose eyes had kindled as he embarked upon a favorite topic, here brought his remarks to an abrupt conclusion. Only Shems-ud-dìn made even a pretense of listening, and in his face was every mark of abstraction. Zeyd and Shibli, on their heels, were talking apart in whispers. Rising, the instructor bowed so low before Shems-ud-dìn that the whole circle of his white turban was seen for a moment, a ring round a scarlet disk, then, with the words, " In thy grace," he stalked off umbrageously toward a group of cypress trees, where others of his kind were sitting in the shade.

Shems-ud-dìn at length observed that the sun was high. Waking out of dreams, he brushed his hand across his eyes.

" The house of the Frank should be astir by this time," he said. " Wilt thou, O my son, come with me thither? "

" Upon my head. . . . Nevertheless, since it is now known that Hassan is not slain, I would fain seek him out, and hear his tale, which must be a strange one."

Shems-ud-dìn gazed on Shibli's brightened countenance, and his eyes were earnest though he seemed to smile. Distressed by that searching look, the youth hung his head and faltered:

"Allah witness, I go with thee gladly—very gladly. It was for afterwards——"

"I did but tempt thee, O my son. I require thee not. But how long wilt thou strive to deceive me?"

He touched Shibli's hand affectionately and would have left him; but the youth ran after, imploring forgiveness. Gently he shook him off, saying:

"Go in peace, my soul. Allah forbid that I should load thee with a grief not thine. Think not I blame thee. Go and hear the story."

CHAPTER XVIII

WHEN Shems-ud-dìn knocked that morning at the door of the Frank's house, it was opened to him immediately. Zeyd had not time to exchange the usual compliments with a sherbet seller, who had his stall higher up the alley, in the shade of a little entry which alone broke the monotony of its high blind walls. Ismaìl, the black doorkeeper, had been on the watch for their coming.

" Is it thou, O my lord? " he exclaimed, grinning welcome. " The hakìm would speak with thy Grace. He is now at meat, but will soon have done. Deign to enter here."

Instead of conducting Shems-ud-dìn as usual through the cool scoured passage out into the court and so up to the sick room, the black opened the door of a chamber adjoining the entrance—a closet sparsely furnished in the Frankish manner, where the unbeliever used to receive those who came to make trial of his skill in medicine. Zeyd thought to pass in with his master, but Ismaìl restrained him by a strong friendly clasp of his shoulder. The door was closed, and Shems-ud-dìn left alone to his meditations.

Set uneasily upon a chair, his feet tucked under him as far as the awkwardness of the contrivance would allow, he took stock of the little room, its cleanness, the tall, spindle-shanked furniture, the mats of some vegetable fiber, and the buzz of flies beneath its vaulted ceiling. Upon a table in one corner stood two wooden boxes linked together by a slack cord. These boxes gave a focus to his contemplation. In the inner chamber of so great a scientist, he supposed them to possess some occult virtue. Yet, all the while he sat gazing on them and on the room in general, he cared not a jot for anything there, but prayed only for the hakìm to come quickly and make known his latest judgment upon Alia.

At last the Frank looked in, coming straight from meat, as a reminiscent munching testified.

"O sheykh!" he poured forth in that rapid, garbled speech of his, which galloped as if to escape from its own inaccuracy. "May thy day be happy and blessed. For thy daughter, alas! the end is very near. Stay with her to-day, I beg of thee. My house is thy house. I go now about my business. In thy grace!"

So saying, and before Shems-ud-dìn could touch his hand or frame an answer, he was gone again. In his place came Mâs, who ushered his master out through the sunny court and up the stairs to the door of the sick room. The fragrance of that room, its cool, sweet air, refreshed Shems-ud-dìn.

"Praise be to Allah!" cried Fatmeh, in response to his formal query. In a posture of triumph, she waved him on toward the bed. "See her smile to welcome her dear father. Is she not almost recovered? Never again did I think to behold her so well, so happy! O light of my eyes! O my pretty one! O life! O happy day!"

As he sat upon a pile of cushions arranged for him by Fatmeh beside the bed, the reasonable speech and ready smile of the beloved came near to persuade Shems-ud-dìn that the physician had lied to him. All day long he sat there, happier than ever since his coming to El Cûds; and that unowned hope which keeps the door of enjoyment locked out fears. Once he even echoed Fatmeh when she praised Allah for the girl's perfect recovery. His intelligence was relaxed, off guard, a plaything for mocking devils, it seemed to him afterwards.

At length, when it wore toward evening, Fatmeh went out for a while, leaving Shems-ud-dìn alone at the bedside. He held the hand of his daughter, a bird's claw for thinness. No word passed till Alia said earnestly:

"O my father!"

Shems-ud-dìn quickened instantly out of his half-abstraction. His brain throbbing with intensity of interest, he answered:

"What is there, O my daughter?"

"There is this, my father: I fear much to die. I fear the great darkness and the loneliness. Thou knowest how I always have feared to be alone in darkness, how I feel a jinni clutch me, and I scream. O my dearest, O Allah, what shall I do in a darkness which has no boundary, in a silence whence no scream is ever heard?"

She clasped her father's arm and clung to it, trembling. Shems-ud-dìn, leaning over her, heartrent by the horror in her dilated eyes, ransacked his brain for words to calm her.

"Take comfort, O beloved!" he whispered. "Doubtless there is a place for thee in the garden of Allah."

"Yes, O my father. Think not I forget all instruction. But that paradise is a shadowy place. It seems to me, as I lie here and think, that a doubt encircles it. It is but a shadow of that sure and glorious one reserved for men. Hear now my prayer, O my father; it is for that I called to thee. When thou, judged righteous, art with the blessed, deign to remember me, thy daughter, and ask of Allah the favor of my presence with thee. The dark-eyed maids will not hate me, for I am thy daughter; and it is allowed thee to ask for a woman dear to thee on the earth."

"Thou art no woman of mine, in that sense——"

"Hush, O my father! Ask only. Make petition. Is not His mercy boundless? Oh, how I have longed to know that place, the talking fruit, the tree, the wondrous birds, and the voice melodious, and the joy in God's presence. Promise to ask for me, and my fear will be much less."

"If Allah will, if at the last day I be judged fit for salvation, then be sure I will fulfill thy petition, O light of my eyes!"

With a sigh of relief, she loosed hold of him and sank back upon the pillows, closing her eyes. It was some time ere she again opened them. Then, meeting her father's troubled gaze, she smiled languidly, almost voluptuously.

"Be not too sorrowful, O my dear! May Allah reward that kind thought of thine which brought me hither. Here is like paradise. It is part of my fear to die that I must leave this pleasant room—of a light subdued, yet how cheerful!—and the pure sweet odors, and the loving tendance. But what matter! All is allotted." She paused before adding in a more detached strain, as though trying to view herself through strange eyes: " Knowest thou, O my father, that, did it please Allah to preserve me in life, I think I should pray thee to give me to this good hakìm and not to Shibli. When I suffer pain, the hakìm needs but to look on me and it is gone. His touch is gentle, and his eyes are not as the eyes of Shibli, but rather resemble thine, O my father——"

She broke off suddenly, for just then the door of the room opened and the hakìm himself entered, followed by Fatmeh and an unveiled woman who also waited upon Alia.

Shems-ud-dìn withdrew. He knew now that the hakìm had told truth when he said that the end was very near. He saw his late torpor of enjoyment, and the still evident delight of Fatmeh, in their true colors, the colors of the sunset hour, the fairest of the day, the gate of night. The sun of a blinding love drew near his setting.

Going down into the court, he spoke with Zeyd and the two old negroes till the hakìm came forth from Alia, when he ran and clutched his raiment.

" Let me talk with thee, O lord of bounty! "

" Willingly. We will go to the housetop; it is pleasant at this hour."

On the housetop, moving in the blaze of the sinking sun, the Frank explained to Shems-ud-dìn, as well as his knowledge of the Arabic would permit, the nature and peculiar symptoms of Alia's malady. It was incurable, he had said so from the first. He had done what man could to relieve the pain of it, and increase by a little the number of her days. There was nothing more on earth that he could do. Even supposing she might live, which was impossible, the mere life deprived of certain organs would be ghastly torture, no blessing, but a very curse.

Shems-ud-dìn, hearing him theorize thus, and mistaking the tenor of his jumbled words, on a sudden wave of longing forgot even Allah Most High. From his sinful heart he cried:

"Save but the life of her, the life alone! She dead, what have I left on earth to care for?"

Almost fiercely, he gripped the wrist of the Frank, repeating:

"Save but the life, O best of physicians, and may Allah bless thee ever!"

But the name of Allah, glaring in that connection, showed him in a flash the vanity, the gross impiety, of his behavior. Heart-humbled, he let go the arm of the Frank. His head drooped, tears filled his eyes.

The Frank beheld his frenzy and the consequent collapse with more of pity than surprise. He said:

"Thou understandest not. I can do nothing more than is done already. Stay here awhile. Let the air refresh thee. I descend once more into the house."

He then embarked upon some statement beyond his command of language to express. Shems-ud-dìn gathered from a word caught here and there that this Frank was censured of other Nazarenes for receiving the girl in his house, even as he himself had earned the reproach of other Muslims by allowing her to lie there. The sheykh could only thank him with tears in his eyes.

The sun's chin touched the outer roofs to westward. On that side, the city seemed of hewn shadow up against a fire; on the other, ruddy light held all the terraces, with shadow only in their crannies which were streets. Shems-ud-dìn, seated on a high roof, was aware vaguely of a conflagration of all heaven. He thought on the last day, when the sun shall drop so near that the brains of the wicked shall boil like water. He remained unconscious of the attendance of Zeyd, the son of Abbâs, who, seeing the Frank descend, had crept up stealthily, not to be defrauded of a moment of that blest companionship which fed his soul.

Not until the sun had long set, and Shems-ud-dìn

had said his prayers, did Zeyd venture to assert his presence by a sigh and a rustling movement.

"Is it thou, O father of kindness?" asked the sheykh dreamily.

And Zeyd, proud to answer to so sweet a name, said:

"It is none other, O my master."

"Do a kindness, O my friend. Go down, I pray thee, and inquire in the house if my daughter wakes and would see me."

"On my head," answered Zeyd, at once rising. It seemed but a second to Shems-ud-dìn ere the same voice said, "Thy daughter sleeps. The Frank has given her a soothing potion."

"Blest are thy tidings. Then I wait here till Mâs shall call me."

CHAPTER XIX

SHEMS-UD-DÌN fell back on reverie. Above the black gauze veil of earth, the stars beat slumberously. Across the terraced roofs came the voice of one singing, with the twang of a lute. The song was all of love. Now it rose to a frenzied howl, now sank to a passionate moan. From time to time, among the hidden ways beneath, a strife of dogs broke out, raged noisily for a space, and then subsided.

A great weariness beset the sheykh—the accumulated claims of all the nights and days when he had shunned repose. Though he wrestled with it, aware that now, more than ever, there was call to watch, little by little that lassitude overpowered him. He beheld the star-flecked sky for a while fitfully, as if a curtain flapped between it and his eyes. Then he saw no more of sky, or stars, or darkness veiling the face of earth.

He dreamed.

He sat again in his shop in the small bazaar, with hands outspread over the brazier. He heard the chime of camel bells. Some one spoke behind him, when, turning, he beheld an afrìt of baleful aspect, having eyes of flame. And what that devil bade him do, that perforce he did, though well knowing that it was against his own soul.

At blush of day he set out from his small white city of the tawny hills, and the people thronged about him, called him holy, cried to him for a blessing. And he blessed them—he, the slave of evil. The welkin rang with laughter of foul fiends.

He stood beneath the dying tree, denouncing Fatmeh as in righteous anger. And as the woman writhed in anguish at his feet, a voice came from within the litter, "Is the woman's sin above thine? Hast not thou recourse to another than Allah, a creature no more potent than this tree?"

He fell down and strove to pray. But his prayer went crooked, turned away from God. That jinni was at his ear, distracting him.

So he arose and went his way through the tainted air. Friends turned to foes. Old friends grinned aside, mocking him.

Then came one who mistook him for a saint—a poor man, good and faithful. He longed to undeceive him, but could not, the devil preventing.

He stood in the smiling court of the Frank's house. He knelt; he prostrated himself; he offered gifts; he prayed to that unbeliever in place of Allah; wide awake to the sin he thus committed, yet constrained thereto by the evil thing possessing him.

"Save but the life! but the life alone!" he cried; and the infidel, though something loath, consented.

Abd-ur-Rahman, Shibli, Hassan—all old friends forsook him. Only that simple one, who believed in him, still clung to him with reverence. The aged Chief of the Learned, all wise men, remonstrated with him. He saw their mouths open and shut, he felt their disapproval; but his mind made nothing of what they said.

"Save but the life!" he cried in their defiance.

He sat in a chamber of the Frank's house and waited, his soul racked with suspense. The chair on which he sat proved an instrument of torture, crushing both his feet.

Suddenly, a man moved in the room with him, supporting something with both hands.

"The life is saved, O sheykh, the life only. See it here before thee."

The speaker turned, revealing the earth-hued face, the eyes of flame, of that same jinni who had beguiled him at the first. His laugh had the rattle of dry bones as he repeated: "Behold what it is, the life only!"

Then he looked and saw two wooden boxes united by a thin cord, which writhed and twisted between them like a living worm. The tops of the boxes also seemed alive, for they rose and fell regularly like the breast of a sleeper. He stared terror-stricken, fixed to that accursed chair. He saw his poor disciple approach the life and lift both hands in admiration of the rare contrivance. He realized the stupendous mockery of the hope, inspired by devils, which had led him on through sin after sin—for this.

Then, as he glowered upon that fruit of evil, the pulse of the barren life grew faint and fainter, the cord more languid in its twistings. In dread lest even that should escape him, by a mighty effort he wrenched himself free of the chair. Men seized him, wrestled with him, but he broke away, crying:

"O Allah, mercy! It is the life."

There came a shock, a flood of darkness. The stars shone above him, among them the waning moon, late risen, like a flower's curled petal. Some one bent over him, grasping his shoulder. A woman's wail came from below, in the house.

"Allah witness, Zeyd and I have striven hard to wake thee, O my master. It is now too late. Thou hearest that voice of woe, the voice of Fatmeh. Peace to the beloved. She is but now dead."

"Praise be to Allah! What is the hour?"

"It nears the dawn, O my master."

"It is seemly that we make arrangements for her burial this day. Allah forbid that I should trespass any longer upon the kindness of this stranger. I will make him a suitable present, and then, having buried the body of my soul, we will return to our own place."

"Spare thyself all concern," said Mâs gently. "Ismaìl, the doorkeeper, is more skilled than we are in the ways of this city. And he values thee above all living men. He will bargain for a plot of ground, and smooth the way of thy grief before thee."

"May Allah give peace to him and to thee! Nevertheless, I shall go with him to direct his judgment."

In all the words of Shems-ud-dìn there was now a note of decision, almost cheerful, much at variance with his recent listless sorrow. Mâs and Zeyd ebn Abbâs marveled at his might of resignation.

CHAPTER XX

IMPELLED more by shame than prudence, Hassan Agha lay perdue with his men two days and nights after his outwitting by the garrison of El Cûds. The hours of sunlight were spent in lounging about the village of Zeyd's wife's relation, sitting smoking in the shade of the olive yards, or under screen of a rock in the wady; glozing over their defeat until, to the mind's eye, it wore the hue of misfortune, and they were no more shamed.

At break of the third day, when Hassan awoke and stretched himself, his host, already afoot, announced his mind to go presently to the city and visit Zeyd, the son of Abbâs. His desire was not, he confessed, so much to see Zeyd himself, who was a poor man like another, as to greet once more that holy one by whom his house was honored, to inquire of his health and obtain his blessing.

"Thy desire is my own," said Hassan, yawning audibly. "Wait a little and we will go together, thou and I and all my people."

A little later, the peasant having mounted a light-colored ass, they rode over the hill, a goodly company. Every one of Hassan's band was there, not excepting the Thief, who instead of boots wore bandages, tied for him by Ali, who boasted some skill in surgery.

"What? You return to school, all of you?" cried a soldier in the city gate. "Is it possible that you need a second lesson?"

Masking discomfort beneath a genial smile, Hassan cried peace on the merry rogue.

The street within was crowded, obliging them to ride slowly in single file. The sun, risen clear of the roofs, was hot overhead; and the honeycomb of whitish stone seemed an oven constructed on purpose to retain and diffuse the heat. It was hotter than high noon, for noon is ever tempered by some breeze.

They rode to the khan and there dismounted, stabling their horses with the aid and blessing of a ragged hostler. The host came forth likewise and blessed them. By Allah, it enlivened all things to behold them once again. What had become of the excellent sheykh, their friend? His horse, his two mules, and the donkey of his companion were yet, they might see, in the stable. But for three whole days, to-day the fourth, he had not been vouchsafed a glimpse of the sheykh himself. True, an old negro whom he knew not—a taciturn black dog—had come yesterday and brought him money on the sheykh's behalf. But he was not one to think only of gain. By Allah, no! He liked to see his patrons each day, to exchange greetings with them, and assure himself they were happy.

"Doubtless we shall find him by the sanctuary," suggested Shibli, in an undertone; whereupon, taking leave of the host, they trooped toward the Sacred Close. In their midst, Zeyd's wife's relation carried a jar of dried fruits and a bag of olives for an offering to the saint's glory.

Outside the circuit hallowed from of yore, near the foot of a flight of steps, sat a very aged man in converse with another not so old. The pair sat cross-legged against the wall of a fair white shrine whose shadow covered them. Hard by, a withered tree veined the ground with deep, blue shade.

"It is the Chief of the Learned!" exclaimed Shibli, with bated breath. Running forward, he did obeisance to the elder of the two seated. The younger rose in acknowledgment of the civility.

"Who is there, O my brother?" quavered the sage, whose eyes were dim. "Who is he that hails me thus by name? My ears detect the footsteps of a crowd. Doubtless they are pilgrims to the sanctuary—none like it under heaven, save only the House of God which is in Mekka. The mercy of Allah upon you, O true believers! Forgive me though I remain seated. I am old and somewhat feeble, O my children."

But when Shibli humbly submitted that they were not come now as pilgrims, but simply in quest of the Sheykh Shems-ud-dìn, that old man put off the divine, exclaiming with interest:

"You seek that good man, that marvel of instruction? You are his companions of the road? Then are you entitled to a second welcome from me. You ask, where is he now? Ah, of that I cannot certify you. Within this hour he left me—he and the poor man who cleaves to him, and a white-beard Ethiopian, his servant—saying he would go and visit his daughter's grave."

"Is the girl then dead and buried?" the Circassians murmured of consternation.

"Have you not heard? Like many of our human ills, it is in truth a blessing. For had Allah granted life to that girl, our friend had deemed her rescued by the Frank, and so been confirmed in an error of which I strove oft to disabuse him, namely: that it can be lawful to frequent an obstinate unbeliever and to put faith in him—aye, even a faith beyond that in one's own kindred, making him the keeper of a young girl that was a virgin, ascribing to him that power of life and death which is the prerogative of God alone. Have we not cause to rejoice that so great and insidious an error is rooted out ere it could corrupt the heart of a man the best that draws breath?

"I praise Allah hourly for His compassion in enforcing the argument which I, His humble bondman, could not persuade our excellent sheykh so much as to hear with tolerance. His mind is changed, thanks to Allah! He now owns his sin. In return, I invited him to lead the morning prayer. . . . Praise to Allah! . . . But what is here? What wouldst thou?"

Zeyd's wife's relation, hearing such heavenly words, and weary of forever carrying a pot of dried fruits and a bag of olives, had laid those gifts at the sage's feet, himself with them in prayer for their acceptance.

"What is this? Thou bringest gifts—thou whose speech is of the poorest! The poor inherit the privileges of the rich, who nowadays have forsworn liberality. From the hand of Allah thou shalt get reward. Hereafter thou shalt taste the fruits of paradise, basking in shade, and to the strains of an exquisite music."

"O Glory! O Holiness! I am thy debtor till the Last Day!" cried the fellâh, at so rich a promise. Snuffling, with streaming eyes, he went after the Circassians.

Once more they plunged into the city's stifled ways.

"This is like hunting a partridge among the hills. 'Here he was a minute since'; and now, behold! he has flitted across the wady. For him but a spread of the wings, for me an hour's rough walking!" muttered Hassan, wiping his brow. For a pace he strode in silence, frowning moodily. All at once he cried out: "Is that an English physician? I think not, by Allah! The English physician swears by his word, but this dog is a cunning liar. In like manner, seeming most upright, making grave promises, did their knowing ones deliver up our land to the Muscovite. May Allah destroy that nation and blot out the remembrance of it from on earth! Behold us perfectly befooled! May Allah burn that infidel! He received the girl into his house, he made a covenant with us to heal her. He took our gifts, and much money from the Sheykh Shems-ud-dîn. And now he has killed the girl. Doubtless he had deflowered her secretly, and so dared not leave her in life."

From further exposition he was diverted by a cry

most bitter, the cry of one struck down by a treacherous blow.

"Woe, woe on me! . . . The pride of my house—that ancient garment! It is made nothing; it is despised, defiled! It is passed from one dog to another! . . . O dishonor! . . . O Lord, let me slay that infidel! O Allah, destroy his house with fire this minute! . . . Him and the black hog, I will kill them both. Have they not earned death? . . . Ah, woe! woe!"

Nesìb the Thief had broken away from the cherishing arm of Ali, his sworn brother, and now stood unsteadily, with hands upraised to a strip of sky, shrieking curses and blubbering by turns. His face was convulsed with anguish. Ali hovered near with soothing words, ready to catch the rocking cripple should he fall.

"Right is with the Thief," cried Hassan loudly. "It is one thing to be fooled by Abd-ur-Rahman—a child of our house; but by an unbeliever, with whom we dealt too honorably, that is quite another. For the name of the Sheykh Shems-ud-dìn, for our own good name, it behooves us to take vengeance. Y'Allah! To his house, O my children."

Already upon the shouting, strange forms had

come about them, strange voices asked of the matter. When, at Hassan's exhortation, they surged onward, a crowd, three parts Christian, of facile sympathizers went with them. The Thief, still weeping passionately, submitted once more to the tender solicitude of his sworn brother. The aged relative of Zeyd ebn Abbâs had disappeared.

They had not far to go. One quiet alley and a short tunnel brought them into the way which led past the door of the Frank. In the manner of a stone rolled downward, they gained momentum from the fact of moving. The murmur of their indignation swelled to a roar.

Between the high, blank walls, one light, one shadowed, a solitary man was seen running for dear life. It was the sherbet seller who, finding his quiet lane the highway of a yelling rout, had forgotten his stall of cooling drinks.

The mob swayed and eddied for a moment ere it broke upon the door of the Frank physician. All who could come at it beat upon that door; many more, out of sympathy, beat the surrounding wall.

"Open, open, O cursed heathen! Down with the door! The door yields not. Bring fire. Who has fire?"

A woman's voice squealed within. The assailants paused to hear what was said.

"What is this, forsooth? Merciful Allah, are these manners? 'A thousand knock-knock-knocks and no salâm aleykûm.' Ismaìl is out. I will not open. I shall tell of you to the hakìm."

At that the hammering, the shouts, and the yells redoubled, till of a sudden some one cried, "Look up!" and all eyes sought the roof line. There, leaning on the parapet, was the hakìm himself. He held a gun, not pointed menacingly, but simply, as it seemed, for their inspection.

"Go, or I shoot!" he cried.

Even as he spoke, a knife whizzed so near as to graze his cheek. The muzzles of a dozen guns commanded him. Then some stones flew up; but by that time he was no more seen.

"Ha, ha! He is an old woman, this great hakìm!" shouted Hassan. "Another kind of English led the fight at Kars. This is no better than some skulking townsman. O shame, to bear the insult of such an one."

Derisive laughter mingled with the howl of execration. But, realizing that the business was like to go beyond a frolic, many Christians and other chance allies began to edge away.

"Bring fire! Burn the door! Make fire the bawwâb!" cried one of the Circassians.

At once the more zealous of his comrades tried to coax a flame by means of foreign matches and rags torn from their own clothing. But already the more lukewarm were dropping off. The sight of some running made others run. The panic became general. Hassan did not hinder the flight. He considered enough had been done for the present to scare the Frank.

"Stop running. Scatter! scatter!" he shouted for their instruction.

In a moment, had the watch appeared, they would have found no mob, but divers groups of men walking inoffensively—nay, timidly—in divers directions. Like a sand storm in the desert of the south, the riot had arisen, raged, and was clean gone, all in a short quarter of an hour.

"Where is our good fellâh? Where Ali? Where Nesìb?" said Hassan to Shibli, who had clung to him throughout the tumult. "Small wonder if some were swept astray by that sudden blast. Allah pardon! Saw man ever the like of it?"

He proceeded to make inquiry of those he saw stationary in the markets, if anyone had seen a tall old man of a noble countenance, attended by one who seemed a beggar, in all respects, saving only that he did not beg. At last one answered:

"I have seen the very man; and with them a lean old negro who kept grinning without mirth," and pointed out which road the three had taken.

CHAPTER XXI

Nesìb the Thief was left before the house of the physician. Unable to run or help himself because of his injured legs, he must have been knocked down and trampled in that panic rush, but for the tender care of Ali, who fought manfully to protect him. But the Thief himself was blind to the danger escaped, blind to everything except his own cruel shame in dishonor. He kept sobbing convulsively, breaking out at intervals into a fit of wild lamentation, which pierced to the very entrails of Ali, who loved him as his soul.

For fear lest troops should come and surprise them, alone and unprotected, on the scene of riot, Ali helped his suffering love to shelter in an archway farther up the alley, and there ensconced him in the seat of the sherbet seller, behind the stall of cooling drinks. Removing a lemon which served as stopper to one of the large bottles upon the board, he poured out drink for his more than brother into a cup that was there, in the hope to soothe him.

Nesìb took the cup, duteously; but, when he would

have sipped thereof, the tide of grief overcame him, and he turned his face to the wall. The cup would have fallen had not Ali caught it. The heartbroken voice of the beloved cut his bones.

" O Allah, kill me. Have I not reached the nadir of infamy? Are not my legs broken, both of them? Was not my hand bit in two of a fat one? Did not earth open and swallow me? Fell not the lot on me that I should lose my horse? O Lord, have I not borne enough already; but must the honor of my house be defiled by infidels, breakers of faith, ravishers, murderers? And now I have lost the knife I can never replace—to no purpose, for it struck him not. O Allah, avenge me quickly, or I die. Ah, woe! woe! woe! "

Ali knelt beside the weeper. He took Nesìb's head upon his breast. Tender as a mother with her sucking babe, he wiped the slaver from mustache and beard; straightened the turban, smoothed the puckered brow; weeping, he also, and saying:

" O the sin of them. May Allah destroy those wicked ones who have brought such grief upon my dear. But say not ' I am helpless,' while thou hast a brother. Is not Ali whole? Are Ali's two legs broken? Is not all that pertains to Ali thine always to command, employ? Has not Ali a knife, own brother to that thou didst throw? See, here; take, examine it; it is thine!"

Nesìb's limp fingers closed upon the knife, and in gazing down at it his face straightened. He seemed attracted by its flashing brilliance. But presently, when Ali thought him comforted, his face knit once more to weeping, and, with a moan, "I cannot stab with it, but only throw it at a venture," he pushed it from him.

"O Allah, look on him. O Lord, punish the miscreants who have made him thus," cried Ali, beside himself.

He caught up the knife and held it close under the eyes of Nesìb, who had turned his face to the sunlight, but saw nothing through the rain of grief.

"See, I hold this knife — I, Ali, thy sworn brother. The knife is thine, I am thy right arm. I abide here with thee; I watch the alley. Whichever comes, the black or his master, I slay with this knife, the knife of Nesìb; with this arm, the arm of Nesìb; in the name of Nesìb, under Allah. So shall thy wrongs be avenged. Art content, O my eyes?"

Nesìb nodded, speechless. He grew calmer after that. For minutes together he watched the sunny lane with scarce a sob; but then the grief which gnawed his vitals would again assert itself, and Ali would break forth again in imprecations, and renew his oath of vengeance.

"See, I pull off my boots," he said. "There shall be no warning, no betraying footstep. The dog shall fall suddenly as by the hand of Allah."

He dragged off the homemade boots of goatskin, which he wore for riding, and set them before Nesìb to perfect assurance.

"Hush! One approaches. I hear the voice of slippers."

Peeping cautiously out, Ali drew back quickly.

"It is the black. He hastens. He has heard of the tumult. Let us hide behind the stall a moment. Quick, I help thee. Y'Allah! He is acquaìnted with the sherbet seller."

"I would fain see him," whispered Nesìb, stifling a sob.

The footsteps paused before the entry, the negro looking for his old acquaintance, but they quickly went on. Ali stole forth, crouching, swift and noiseless as a leopard to the spring.

The Thief heard a gurgled cry, then three long groans, ere Ali crept back out of the sunshine, and placed in his hands the dagger, warm and wet.

Still sobbing a little, reminiscently, Nesìb took the

dagger and surveyed it lovingly, stroking and fondling it in his lap.

"It is finished. Art content, O beloved?"

"May thy goods increase, O Ali, O my dear brother!" murmured the Thief, still gloating on the bloody knife. Then, on a sudden prompting, he stretched out his arms and caught Ali to his breast in a passionate embrace.

It was Ali's turn to weep convulsively. They clung together, sobbing for joy in their mutual devotion.

"Now let us go, O delight," murmured Ali, at length. "One beheld the deed. He was afar off and he fled. It may be he will tell others."

"I am ready," replied the Thief, wiping the dagger within the breast of his raiment.

Just then a woman's shriek rent the air, giving them pause. Ali whispered:

"They have found the dead pig. Wait a little, O my soul. Let us once more hide behind the stall."

The sound of lamentation continued but a little while. They heard a man's voice give directions, followed by the slam of a door. Then all was still.

A minute longer they crouched in hiding. Then Ali helped his injured love to rise. Nesìb's arm round Ali's neck, Ali's arm about Nesìb supporting him, they emerged into the sunlight.

They had not accomplished many steps from their retreat, when the sherbet seller, returning to his stall, accosted them.

"A happy day, O my uncles! Saw you aught of the great battle that was here awhile ago? Why ask! Thy friend is injured. Ah, Allah knows the wickedness of some people. A drink, now, flavored of rose, or tamar-hind, or lemon, would refresh his honor." He ran to his stall and returned with a cup and bottle. "Nay, take it as a gift; ennoble me. The breeze has sprung up, but one feels it not just here. I present the breeze and the shade of trees and the bubbling waters. Do but sip, I entreat thee; it is paradise."

CHAPTER XXII

FROM visiting his daughter's grave, Shems-ud-dîn sauntered round by the walls of the city till he came to that rocky steep, at the top of which he had preached to the negroes. He took a path that ran down slantwise into the wady, and the embattled walls were soon lost to sight. Mâs and Zeyd, the son of Abbâs, followed him implicitly, though at a discreet distance, and when at length he crossed his legs in the shade of a little bluff, they took example from him and did likewise.

The sheykh's face was coldly serene as he gazed on the sunburnt rocks, among which rose ancient tombs strange of shape. He had sat there in peace about an hour when a shout disturbed him. It fell from the rocks above, and ruffled his countenance as a stone the surface of a pool. Other shouts ensued. He recognized the voice of Hassan, the laugh of Shibli. Men came scrambling down the rocks. With scarce an effort he admitted the call for patience, and his brow smoothed again.

"Allah comfort thee, O sheykh," cried the foremost of the Circassians. "May the wound to thy soul be healed. May that treacherous Frank perish, his house be burnt, his parents dishonored. Already we have done something to avenge thee. In sh' Allah, we have made him quake a little."

"I hear words of no meaning," said Shems-ud-dìn, who had risen. "What intend you by such talk?"

Dismayed by the stern front opposed by their saint to news they had deemed most welcome, the men herded, silent and abashed, pending the arrival of their chief who, being elderly and stiff at the joints, used caution in the descent from rock to rock. At length Hassan, breathless, slid down among them.

"O beloved, how great the grief. How I sorrow with thee," he exclaimed in accents of condolence. "By Allah, it seems ten years since last I saw thee."

"It is in truth some days, and thou art welcome, O my dear. But say, what is this of which thy companions prate—some outrage done to the hakìm, my benefactor?" Shems-ud-dìn stood erect, severely questioning. His eyes met Hassan's steadily.

The Guardian of the Frontier hung his head as at the Last Day. But soon recovering, he told the story of the riot, representing it as a game, a little pleasantry at the expense of one who had deserved much worse at their hands; for had he not obtained their presents by a false pretense?

"As for naming him thy benefactor, O scion of a noble house, I grieve to hear thee thus exalt the dirt beneath thee. Hast thou not paid him as though he had performed his covenant? Surely he is thy debtor. Remains the affront to thee and all of us here."

"I laugh for pity," said Shems-ud-dìn, with a fleeting smile. "In the case of some other than myself, I might laugh with amusement, for the thing is ludicrous. Is it not a stock expedient with the provokers of mirth to throw the punishment for crime upon some good man and simple, most innocent thereof? I alone have sinned, and lo! you visit my sin upon this physician, whose fault has been excess of kindness. Shall I not own obligation? I offered the half of my fortune; I struck no bargain with him beforehand; he could have claimed the half of me. Yet, when it came to the reckoning, he asked but his just due, and named all the items in account. Which of you, in his place, would have dealt so gently with a stranger?

"You assail his house, assault, affright him. By what right, I demand to know? Are you, and not I, in account with him? Hear the words of Allah. You know the korân, ' He that shall err, shall err only for his own soul, nor shall any laden be charged with another's burden '; and again, ' The fate of every man is tied about his neck.' By what right, then, do you meddle with the things which concern me only? Is your sympathy for me so great that, seeing I have sinned, you must sin yourselves more abominably? . . . Go, O Zeyd. Speed to the house of that worthy infidel. Express to him my regret for the disturbance caused to his house by these, my too ardent sympathizers."

" Ready, O my master." Zeyd moved to obey, but laggingly, and with the mien of one much loath. For Zeyd prized the eloquence of Shems-ud-dìn above all jewels. The fine words, accurately pronounced by the scholar, sang of love to his soul, which languished as a bride expectant. And never had Shems-ud-dìn spoken as now he spoke, with such authority, such inspiration in the choice of fitting words. Zeyd grudged that feast to the Circassians, to Mâs, to fickle Shibli. He alone could quite appreciate it; and he must go. He went very slowly.

The other listeners, disconcerted by the attitude of their saint, still more by an unwonted smile which flickered round his lips, had not a word to reply. Sarcasm was a weapon they all feared, and it was the weapon least expected from so mild a man. But what they took for sarcasm in this instance was, in truth, but the natural expression of one new-weaned from earthly longing, whose mind now dwelt with Allah and behèld the things of earth from an immeasurable height.

He went on to speak to them of his own sin, quoting, " Man prays for evil, as he prays for good, for man is unthinking "; when all personal feelings became lost in pure admiration of his golden gift. His language grew so refined, his mind soared so near to heaven, that they, his hearers, could only gasp and praise the Lord.

" Hear the supreme khatìb. O my soul, the heavenly preacher," panted one and another.

All at once there burst a sobbing cry from out the rocks above, the cry of one at the pang of sensual enjoyment.

" Ah, ah! his lips are gold. Gems shower from them. O my eyes! O Allah One and Unaccompanied! "

The preacher paused and glanced upward. A disreputable tarbûsh, garnished with a dirty rag by way of turban, peeped above a neighboring crag.

" O Zeyd," cried the sheykh severely, " art thou

not sped then? Since it irks thee to do my bidding, Mâs goes instead of thee."

"Nay, I go, O my lord." The face and shoulders, half the form of Zeyd, popped up very suddenly. "But oh, what words! What treasure! O blessed day!" He was seen to scale the rocks with alacrity.

His master smiled; and even in the moment of displeasure there had been that about his mouth and in his eyes which showed that the mind despised its own vexation.

Shems-ud-dìn continued to speak of sin, and the need of good works, and of the judgment, when a book shall be given to each of the sons of men wherein he shall read his own account for good or evil.

The sun of noon burned overhead, yet none stirred to escape its rays. Above the wady, a gash in the rugged landscape, a hawk hovered, seeming motionless. Faint sounds came wafted from a village on the yonder steep, of one color with the rocks to which it clung.

At length a growth of noise above them excited curiosity. Some of the circle rose and scanned the height.

"Ma sh' Allah!" cried Hassan. "A bird must

have carried the fame of thy discourse into the city, O beloved, for much people watch us from the rocks."

"Allah! What was it flashed there, behind that stone?"

"By the Korân, there are men all about us, moving secretly."

Hassan Agha tugged at his white mustache.

"Let us be walking," he commanded. "Show no concern, my children, nor fight, for the foe is numerous. With thy leave, O beloved, we will return to the city together."

Shems-ud-dìn, undismayed, took the hand held out to him, and walked with his old friend slowly along the path which wound upward among the rocks.

"Stand, all of you."

From beside an ancient tomb two soldiers stood forth suddenly, barring the way. At that Hassan railed:

"What ails you, O my dears? Has the sun addled your wits that you venture to command this holy man, a great one, no less than brother to the renowned Milhem Pasha, whom Allah preserve."

Soldiers were now all about them, joking good-naturedly. There had been no resistance, and they were grateful, for it was very hot.

"Allah witness how I grieve for you," laughed

one in whom Hassan recognized the Bimbashi Muhammed. " But to sift the innocent from the guilty is not our business. That belongs to the judge; let him see to it. By Allah, thou art out of luck, old fox. This is no jesting matter like ours of the other night."

The man held his tongue, for a superior officer now approached them, scrambling up from below. Hassan scanned the features of the newcomer eagerly, but sighed; it was not Abd-ur-Rahman.

" With what are we charged? " he inquired, scorn born of indignation making the words a sword thrust.

" By my life, I know not for certain," came the light rejoinder. " There is talk of a riot and a man slain, an old negro, the slave of a Jew of some sort, who is an English subject. It is a word from the English consul that has fluttered the Mutesarrif; we do not move so quickly in the cause of true belief. A sin, as my brother—who is religious—rightly says. But what would you? The infidels—Jew and Christian—outnumber us here in the proportion of ten to one; and they have strong and unscrupulous protectors in the Powers of Europe. To keep the mastery we must sometimes throw a crumb. May Allah cleanse you of the charge."

Shems-ud-dìn heard these words and many others; but their purport remained vague to him. He perceived only, and with a species of exultation, that he was called upon to exhibit that strength in resignation which now informed his whole being. On the broad road, beneath the echoing gate, in the rough-paved streets, he heard the murmur of a crowd, restless, inquisitive. Here it surrounded them, there dropped behind. Of a sudden, in a sunless place, a man cried suddenly:

"O Hassan Agha! O holy Shems-ud-dìn! O Allah most high! What thing do we behold?" The voice went along with them, shouting questions, till at length it fawned in entreaty. "O lords of kindness! O soldiers brave and good! Take us also, for the crime is ours."

"Since thou and thy friend desire the scourge, the prison, even death, perhaps, who am I to gainsay thee, O father of two bad legs?" laughed the captain of the guard; and Nesìb the Thief, sustained of Ali, came in among them.

At the door of the Mehkemeh, several of the curious slipped in with the prisoners, for these were too plentiful for the soldiers to keep strict count, though the trial was ordered to be secret.

The hall, murmurous with their voices, struck dark on Shems-ud-dìn. It was some time ere he could see the likeness of the judge; but at length he discerned a fat man seated in apparent dejection upon a dais, a scribe before him, and on his right hand one but little leaner, who wore Frankish clothes beneath his fez, and appeared in the best of spirits—a servant of the English consul, it was whispered.

CHAPTER XXIII

Yûsuf Effendi, Câdi of El Cûds, was sullen and discontented, in the mood to strike his best friend. An hour ago a scribbled note from the Mutesarrif had dashed the complacency with which he sat listening to a case of fraud between a Jew and a Greek, having garnered more than the sum sued for in bribes from either party. The court had to be cleared, judgment given hastily, when he loved deliberation and the dainty quibbling of the pleaders before him. Other cases, no less profitable, had to be adjourned—rich plaintiffs and defendants driven forth with the money in their hands; and all in favor of a cause prejudged by his superior—a political cause for which no gifts could be received, no advocates employed—at the behest of an unclean beast, the English consul.

"It is imperative that the delinquents die ere sunset. Make some show of trial. Shut the door."

There was no evading the clear orders of one on whose will he depended for rank and honor. Yet he would fain have shirked the responsibility, for in a fat and easy way he feared God. Though he received gifts, of course, from all and sundry, in giving judgment he knew no influence save the rights of the case.

He was no roving, conscienceless official to level foul with clean, but a man of fixed abode and consequent respectability, who, though urbane in his dealings with the infidels, esteemed them no more than dogs in his way to business. This charge to do the dirty work of a Frank humiliated him. It galled his pride, also, to have to endure the familiarity and regard the hints of a low-born Christian of his own city, who actually had the impudence to sit at his right hand, in the place of honor. Yûsuf would fain have invoked the Mûfti, as usual in cases of religious difference; but, knowing the anxiety of the governor that the trial should be hid especially from the mosque authorities, he dared not do so. He groaned in soul:

"O day of evil! Is it not enough that I, who had ever enjoyed the security which belongs to respect, have been robbed of my rents, stripped, and foully insulted within this week? Must I afterwards jeopardize my salvation at the call of the wicked?"

The inflow of so many prisoners as almost to fill the hall caused the judge to discern faint rays of hope. It could be necessary to condemn only a few of them;

and the rest, in the rapture of escape, might well make thank offerings to their preserver.

He turned from converse with the noisome beast beside him to whisper in his scribe's ear:

"Write: How many are to die? and address to his Highness the Mutesarrif."

The scribe straightway wrote as commanded, while the Nazarene, sweetly smiling, craned his neck in a vain attempt to spy what was written. The note was given to an attendant who, crying, "Oäh! Oäh!" pushed his way to the door.

Then, having enjoined silence, Yûsuf began to harangue the multitude, without looking, in a manner of abstract reprobation, heedless of the impatience of the consul's representative and the rising murmur in the court, until an answer was received; when he took breath just long enough to decipher:

"As many as you judge fit. The wild beast is bloodthirsty—a danger unless we glut him. At sight of this, tear up."

Upon that, in a few words, he closed his lecture on jurisprudence, which had served its turn.

"In mercy let the trial now begin," murmured the Offense at his side pointedly.

"Interrupt not, I beseech thee," rejoined Yûsuf, giving sting for sting. He could not look upon those true believers he was doomed to wrong. Shame dropped a curtain at the edge of the dais. With eyes downcast upon a chaplet with which his hands kept toying, he asked, " Who accuses? "

" I am he," returned the Christian; " on behalf of the illustrious consul of Her Britannic Majesty, and as representing one Jurjus Mekkuswell, a missionary doctor, who is a British subject."

" Against whom, and of what nature, the accusation? "

" Against divers Circassians, colonists, from Jebel Ajlûn, for attacking the house of the hakìm and murdering one Ismaìl, his servant. But principally against the Sheykh Shems-ud-dìn El Attâr, likewise from Jebel Ajlûn, who instigated the said attack, the said murder."

" The Sheykh Shems-ud-dìn El Attâr, is he present in the court? " cried the judge, without looking up from his beads.

" Present," answered a full, clear voice.

" Are there any Circassians present in the court? "

" No need to ask, O lord! The court is full of them," murmured the scribe at his feet.

" It is well. The accused are before us. Let the English hakìm testify against them."

At that the Christian showed annoyance, calling

the demand vexatious, unnecessary. The hakìm had made deposition before the consul, which was quite sufficient. Naturally, after the outrages committed against him, he was not calm enough to appear in public. To what purpose on earth should he come? The crime was indisputable, for it was the talk of the whole city. And the prisoners had made themselves so notorious on former occasions, that any lad out of the street could identify them.

The Câdi appeared dissatisfied with the representations of his loathsome colleague. He would not submit without a wrangle. But at length, after prolonged whisperings, he said aloud:

"Good. Then what witness have you?"

"We have a capital witness—none like him!—a certain vender of cooling drinks, who saw all that befell. He has been examined already before the consul, but is now in this court, at your Excellency's pleasure. His name is Mûsa. If it please you, hear him."

"Call Mûsa the sherbet seller," murmured the Câdi wearily; and "Mûsa the sherbet seller" was called on every hand.

A Muslim of middle age pushed forward through the crowd. He bent double before the dais.

"To hear is to obey, O majesty!"

"Do thou interrogate him, O khawâjah," said the Câdi bitingly. "Thou, it seems, art conducting this trial."

"Allah forbid that I should usurp any function of your Grace!" murmured the supple Christian. Nevertheless he proceeded to question the witness, while the judge told his beads sulkily, never lifting his eyes.

Did the witness recognize among the men in court a certain sheykh who had been wont to go often to the house of the English physician, for the reason that his sick daughter lay there?

Most certainly he did, and was glad to see the excellent man in life and health, after the grievous blow he had sustained in the loss of his daughter.

It was not the answer required by the consul's delegate; but he swallowed his disconcertion and proceeded.

"What kind of a man did the witness consider him to be?"

"The very best kind of man. No less than a saint, by Allah."

Stung by a cackling noise in the throat of the judge, the Nazarene thundered:

"O lying dog! Thou didst tell another tale to

the consul's excellency. Thou hast made oath that he was concerned in the riot."

"No, no, by thy leave, O dear lord; I said not that he knew aught of the riot, but that they who made the tumult might have been his companions."

"Are they here present, those rioters?"

"Allah knows! In so great a crowd there may be some of them. But my eyes see some who are very certainly innocent. That man there, who leans upon his neighbor, is one of the victims, having both his legs injured in the battle. I know well, for he is a customer of mine and refreshed himself at my stall afterwards. And the Sheykh Shems-ud-dìn, he is very innocent; and the negro Mâs, his servant——"

"Liar! Dolt! Madman! He is the chief offender, that Sheykh Shems-ud-dìn! Get thee gone, O perjured wretch! May Allah destroy thee!" The Christian turned from denouncing the recreant to murmur suavely in the Câdi's ear, "It is my error. This witness ought to have been examined privately. He dares not to speak truth in the hearing of the prisoners for fear of vengeance, since they all know him."

"What? Is it finished already? Have you no other witness?" Again that strange sound was heard in the throat of the judge.

"No, O Excellency; but the charge is clear, the case proven beforehand. Wilt thou not give judgment?"

Yûsuf Effendi feigned not to hear the suggestion. Since it was God's will that he, the Câdi of El Cûds, should be chained to an ape, the shackles should not gall him only. The monkey, too, must feel them on the raw. There were yet some hours till sunset.

"It behooves first to hear the defense," he said languidly; and then sat in silence for some minutes.

Peace had fallen on the court. The prisoners and their guards, tired of standing, all sat now upon the floor.

At length the Câdi, still intent on his beads, murmured sleepily:

"Who is chief among you reprobates, let him speak."

At that there arose some whispered debate among the accused, as though to adjust the preëminence. But soon a clear voice uttered:

"O Excellency, what can be said? I am an old man, and my life is of small account. If one here must die, be mine the lot, and let all these go free. It is the will of Allah, unto Allah praise! Is it not better for a man to die being innocent than being guilty? For Allah is just and compassionate; He will correct the balance. But thou, O my son, consider, I beseech thee, how heinous thy sin is! Thy mind is bent, not to minister justice, but to slay. Thou hast not even recited the charge against me. The hand of the infidel is well seen in thy behavior. A tempter grins at thy right ear. Beware, O judge, how thou pervert judgment; for thyself shalt be judged and shalt wander blind at the Last Day!"

Yûsuf did not look up nor cease from telling his beads. He said irritably:

"Shall the caitiff rebuke his judge? Smite his mouth some of you! . . . Let a second now speak, and see that he be not insolent."

This time a rougher voice, using the speech of the common soldiers with an accent like the Turkish, declaimed:

"O most Excellent, I am a Circassian, chief of those who migrated to this land years ago from the yoke of the Muscovite. The Sultàn Abdul Mejìd named me Guardian of the Frontier by express firmàn. Great honor had we in those days, I and my companions, both at Istanbûl the mighty and on arrival in this land. Then men vied one with another in kindness toward us. Power stood by us like a sworn brother. But to-day all is changed. No man regards us any more. I have served the Sultàn faithfully at my post these many years. I have swept back the Bedû from the borders of this province, as one strikes the dust off a friend's robe. I have furthered every effort of the government. And for what reward? To be denied a few rifles, a sufficiency of ammunition, by your garrison. To be treated worse than you treat the beggar in your gates. To be haled before your Grace this day upon a charge I comprehend not!

"Truly the faith of those in authority is but for a day, and their obligation but as shifting sand. Let none deceive himself to think it lasting, lest he stand as I stand now, ashamed in his old age."

Overcome with emotion, the speaker paused; to resume shortly:

"What would be said of a man who thus used his servant? Now I care not though we die, I and my companions, for death is not more bitter than has been our undeceiving. We have sinned oft and grievously, and it may be we deserve to die. But put to death the upright and illustrious Shems-ud-dìn, that friend of all the learned, dear to Allah, and may all thy bones rot painfully joint by joint! May all men spew at sight of thee! May thy children——"

A mighty uproar drowned the curse. The whole court rose as one man. The Câdi bounced to his feet, mouthing, gesticulating, a-tremble with rage and terror.

"Dog!" he yelled. "Be silent, madman! Pluck his tongue out, scourge him, flay him! Ho, you soldiers! Is it fear holds you there idle?"

At the taunt a dozen soldiers ran and seized on Hassan, who had stood his ground defiantly.

Not until the wretch was clearly powerless did Yûsuf Effendi venture to meet his eyes. The effect of that glance was magical. The fat and sleepy Câdi turned a maniac. He shrieked and shrieked again, in convulsions as if his robe had been poisoned.

CHAPTER XXIV

"THEY are impostors, robbers, murderers. They shall die, every one of them. They robbed me—me, the Câdi—of the moneys I had collected from my lands. Two of them. Two devils! I hold one: where is his brother? Aha, I see him. He skulks yonder. Bring forward that man of the thick beard —he who stoops behind the tall one. Bring him hither to beside his fellow. Hold fast his arms."

Nesìb, the Thief, was dragged to the foot of the dais. He screamed for the pain such rough usage inflicted on his wounded legs; while Ali, withheld from following him, screamed yet more lustily. When the judge stooped down and deliberately spat in his face, Nesìb's screams increased to a very death shriek, which was echoed of Ali in the crowd behind.

"O Allah! O crown of infamy! He bit my wrist, and now he spits on me. O woe! woe!"

Hassan Agha, subjected to the same insult, only sneered and craved the freedom of one hand to wipe his face, which was denied him.

Somewhat allayed by this ceremony, the wrath

of the judge put on the garb of reason. He had no longer the slightest compunction in sentencing those Muslims to a shameful death.

"In the name of Allah, you deserve to die, all of you. For not one misdeed, but a thousand are proved against you. These two men here before me, for their more abominable crimes, shall be strangled and left unburied. On the rest of you I have mercy: they will be shot. Subject to the will of the Mutesarrif, our Sultàn's shadow on this land—whom may Allah preserve. In the name of Allah, gracious, compassionate, it is decreed."

At that went up a bitter cry from all the multitude, but especially from those inquisitives who for pastime had thrust their way into the court. In hopes to save their comrades and one another, Nesìb and Ali each yelled his confession of guilt. But the uproar sufficed to drown individual voices. Curses, lamentations, prayers, mingled discordantly, while the soldiers struck here and there at the noisiest, felling some of them and fetching blood from mouths and noses. The hall of judgment wore the aspect of a shambles. From the dais beside the judge, the plump and smiling Christian gloated on the scene.

The disorder was at its height when a door at the

back of the hall opened, letting in a ray of sunlight upon the hindmost of the crowd.

"Shut the door," shrieked the Câdi, in sudden terror.

Instantly he was obeyed. But some one had entered. The soldiers, saluting, cleared a way for Abd-ur-Rahman Bey to the foot of the dais.

The face of the young man was haggard and hard set. At glad cries of his own name, he glanced this way and that unseeingly.

"Abd-ur-Rahman! It is himself—Abd-ur-Rahman. O son, preserve thy father. Save thy friends."

He stepped upon the dais and, totally disregarding the cringe of the consul's dragoman, addressed the judge without a compliment:

"What is this, O Effendi? Why these cries to me for help? Surely one of thy discrimination has perceived that these men are guiltless of the crime imputed to them?"

"By what right, O my eyes, dost thou use this tone with me?" snapped the Câdi angrily, darting an uneasy glance at the besetting Nazarene. "These men are guilty of riot and bloodshed, violent robbery and rebellion. They die, and their doom is righteous. It is my last word."

"Then it is a bad day for thee, O my dear. For

know that among these men is my father, a reverend and most learned sheykh of the religion, whose death all Islâm will deplore. He is, moreover, the beloved brother of Milhem Pasha whose power, as thou knowest, is considerable. And further, these Circassians are under direct protection of the government, as can be proved by a reference to the archives. My uncle Milhem Pasha knows this and has procured renewal of the firmàn concerning them. But yesterday he informed me in writing that a grant of new rifles will shortly be made to them, and in the same letter named them his friends. Reflect a little, I entreat thee, O my soul."

The confidence of Yûsuf staggered. For the moment he knew not what to murmur, where to look. The chief of those soldiers who herded the prisoners came to his relief, laughing:

" Believe him not, Yûsuf. It is a generous lie to save these poor people whom he knew of old. And really, in thy place, I would spare the most of them. More than once have I heard him deny the truth of a report which made yon old man his father."

" Nay, it was then that I lied," cried Abd-ur-Rahman, as if in pain. " I was ashamed of one so poor in seeming, so old-fashioned, so simply pious. So I lied—mad that I was!—and denied my father."

"Then wert thou dirt, a thing to spit on. But praise to Allah, I believe thee not," said the officer, turning on his heel.

"It is that, thou liest to save them," said the Câdi, with restored confidence.

Then Abd-ur-Rahman called God to witness. He threatened, entreated, reasoned, all in vain.

Still "It is hard to believe," shrugged the Câdi, smiling.

"The men are already condemned. It is clearly proved against them," said the Nazarene, at his ear, as a needed reminder.

"Then it is the worse for thee, O Yûsuf Effendi," cried Abd-ur-Rahman, in a fury. "I go hence to the French telegraph; and if before the sun sets, the wrath of Milhem Pasha is not loosed against all the Mutesarrifate of El Cûds, may Allah strike me dead this minute."

With that and a moan, "O my father!" he pushed his way out. Once more the door opened, admitting a sunbeam, then closed again. A hush was on the seated crowd. The Câdi returned to his beads for countenance, his downcast face in the shadow of a great perplexity. The cheerful Christian whispered at his ear:

"Had that old man been in truth his father,

would he not have run and embraced him? Not once did he look toward him, for I observed closely. Moreover, this sheykh resembles not in the least a man learned and of a good house."

For the first time cordial with his vile associate, Yûsuf agreed.

"By Allah, the right is with thee. But who is this Milhem Pasha? His name is known to me. What is his exact position at this day?"

"Who knows? Doubtless he is a pasha like another. Every youth cries up his own house."

Still the Câdi was ill at ease. He dared not dismiss the prisoners for execution, yet had nothing more to say to them, having given sentence. He desired earnestly to be rid of the spy at his side, who crippled him with a sense of undesirable publicity.

Seeing the beast yawn and look sleepy, he begged him with all customary blessings to retire and seek repose. The trial was ended, the doom pronounced. The rest consisted in a few formalities unworthy of his assistance. He or his Excellency the consul could come after sunset to the Tower to see the bodies.

The Christian did not need much persuasion. He had fulfilled the commands of his lord and was very sleepy. Yûsuf Effendi bowed low with a profusion of blessings, which changed to as great a profusion of curses when he was gone.

To refresh his wits, he then bade the scribe make coffee, for which all necessaries were at hand. He lighted a cigarette and smoked it pensively, still toying with his chaplet. The prisoners, thankful for a respite, sat in groups upon the floor, exchanging cigarettes with their guards, smoking, and chatting together very peacefully. Only Shems-ud-dìn kept aloof with Mâs the negro. He missed but one thing, to grieve for it, and that was the soiled headgear and old striped cloak of Zeyd ebn Abbâs. The whole succession of events and characters—judge and sentence, soldiers and prisoners, the coming and going of his only son—made but a speck on his mind, where it floated like a tiny boat that frets upon a great calm sea.

At length, after two cups of coffee, Yûsuf whispered to his scribe:

" Write to the Mutesarrif, asking of what rank, what influence is Milhem Pasha, uncle to the young Abd-ur-Rahman? Add, for his Excellency's guidance, that the question concerns the trial."

The note dispatched, he sat inactive, looking down at his beads, till came the answer:

" Since two days he is Grand Wazìr; I have the

news this hour from a private source. If the culprits are under his protection, kill anyone else in the world, but spare them, or thou art ruined, I with thee. Let no eye behold this writing."

All things swam before the Câdi's eyes. Had Abd-ur-Rahman spoken truth, he was indeed in a nice dilemma.

CHAPTER XXV

SCOURGED by his master's mild reproof of him for loitering, Zeyd needed no second reminder to make haste. With the bounds of a goat he scaled the rocks and ran along by the foot of the city wall. The noble words which had enthralled him to forget duty boomed in his brain, making earth heaven, wrapping him in a cloud of gorgeous imagery. As he neared the gate, a band of soldiers marched out silently, attended by a little horde of ragamuffin Jews and Christians. The arrow of the sheykh, he scarce perceived them, intent only upon the will of his master, to do which was in itself a rapture. He measured not his pace on such an errand, and it was with surprise, when nearing the house of the Frank physician, that he found sweat streaming from every pore.

He knocked thrice before anyone answered, and then it was not Ismaìl's voice, but that of the serving maid, which smote his ear:

"Who is there? What would you?"

"It is I, Zeyd ebn Abbâs, having an errand to the khawâjah."

"Art thou alone out there? Is it sure there are none beside thee?"

"By Allah, it is sure. Who else on earth should there be?"

"Then enter and behold the work of thy master. O day of my grief! O wicked day! . . . The hakìm is not in the house. It is now two hours since he went forth. Allah grant they have not killed him also, the wicked ones!"

Thus lamenting, she let Zeyd in. He dared not, for his soul's weal, glance at her unveiled face. Her sobs and reproaches vexed him. They called for retort, but he dared not parley with the mistress of so great attractions.

"Y' Allah! Come and see what thy master has done for us, his benefactors! The hakìm will soon return, in sh' Allah, and then thou shalt hear truth for once in life. It is two hours since he went out to the house of the consul. Aha, a proper vengeance shall overtake thee and thy master and all thy race of dogs!"

She dragged him through into the court. She had the strength of a jinni. Her clutch rent his clothing, which had been ragged enough before. Yet he dared not offer resistance lest, at touch of her, desire should master him.

A second voice of woe assailed his ears. It came from the shadowed side of the yard, from out a vault, of which the door stood open.

"Go in! Look!" shrieked his conductor, dragging him to that doorway.

Zeyd strove after the superior smile of one who humors a madwoman, but his look changed quickly to horror and his hands flew up. There, within, upon a low couch, lay the form of Ismaïl the doorkeeper, stiff in death, the face fixed in a travesty of its wonted kindly grin. The brow seemed to have shrunk away from beneath the turban, the cheeks had sunken; the white beard seemed a growth independent of the chin it fastened on. It was no longer the man, simple yet so wise, whom Zeyd had known and revered, but something derisive, harsh, and terrible, a menace and a curse.

Beside the corpse lay Fatmeh on her face, weeping bitterly. The girl who had admitted Zeyd pushed past him and kicked the prostrate one again and again, then, kneeling, beat and pinched her unmercifully, screaming:

"Weep! Weep! By the Gospel, I will make thee weep, O cause of misfortune to the house that sheltered thee. Foul daughter of a Muslim, weep louder, louder! Oh, if all you Muslimûn were made on the pattern of him who lies there, then earth would be a different place! Cease not to weep, lest I tear thy eyes."

In the frenzy of her spite, she had forgotten Zeyd. When he flung her back by main force, she looked on him with blind eyes a moment. Then with the hiss of an angry serpent she strove to scratch his eyes, spitting venomously.

"May Allah blind and maim thee! All shall die—thou and thy wicked sheykh, and this woman, and the rest of you—all—all! My lord went to the consul—the consul, hear you? And the end of all of you is concerted, if not accomplished. . . . Ah, devil! What wouldst thou? Let go; let go, I say! O Allah! O Blessed Lord!"

Anger had driven from Zeyd's mind every thought of goodness. He saw only the charms of the woman, remembered only her brutality to Fatmeh, and the affronts she had put upon himself. With clenched teeth and blazing eyes, he was working to master her when the voice of the Frank called without. In the same minute she ceased struggling and he let go.

Then, too late, Zeyd remembered that he had come on an errand of apology; and he hung his head. Was he himself any better than the Circassians?

Truly, a man uninspired was no more master of his own impulses than is a sword in a strong hand. Crest-fallen and ashamed, Zeyd went and humbled himself before the physician. He tried to give his message. But the unbeliever would not listen, making moan in his own fashion, which was not that of the son of an Arab, with gestures and a bitter cry, but simply a sardonic grinning and muttering, the while his hands trembled, clasped and unclasped nervously.

"Begone! Walk! Go out of my house! Have I not seen enough of thee and thy master? A good return—is it not?—for all I did for the girl. He brings the city against me. He kills my doorkeeper, the best of men. He shall be severely punished, word of an Englishman! The consul says so. But as for me, I lose my appointment. The society will not retain me after all this. I have to thank thy master for much—very much. I think so indeed. He is a good man, not so? Excellent! Ah, ha, ha! . . . Speak not! Begone! Walk! And take the woman with thee. Let me see the end of all of you!"

There was no reasoning with a creature so plainly distraught. "Begone!" he kept repeating, till at last Zeyd renounced all further attempt to pierce his understanding and said, a little irritably:

" To hear is to obey."

Zeyd went back into the death chamber, murmured " Peace to the upright! " by the corpse of the kind old negro, and taking Fatmeh by the hand raised her and led her forth. By the outer door of the house stood the weeping maidservant. She opened for them and, as they passed out, struck Fatmeh such a blow beneath the shoulders that she groaned and fell forward, coughing violently. Zeyd thought her stabbed. He turned to take vengeance, but the door was shut.

Fatmeh lay upon the cobbles of the narrow lane, groaning and coughing by turns; while Zeyd raised hands of denunciation against that house of sin, calling to Allah for justice upon her murderers. No help, no human form, was at hand. The accustomed seat of the sherbet seller was empty.

Soon, however, to his vast relief, Fatmeh rose up, expressing her readiness, and he led her to the khan.

It was the heat of the day when no one fares abroad who can help it. Those they met were too indolent to take note of the tousled raiment of a woman or the mad mutterings of a man, who at a glance seemed mere beggars.

On arrival at the khan the host put many anxious questions to them out of the kindness of his heart.

He was more than repaid by the thrill of Zeyd's narrative.

"Ma sh' Allah!" he exclaimed at the end. "It is not good to frequent unbelievers. The sheykh—dear, righteous man!—he thought no evil—that is known. And yet it was not good. I myself could have informed him harm would come of it."

He readily undertook to lodge Fatmeh with his own women.

While they yet stood talking in the doorway, an ass, saddled and bridled, was led out from the adjoining stable. It was followed by an aged fellâh, who gave a coin to the hostler. The fellâh then bestrode the beast, groaning like a camel with the exertion. Zeyd, recognizing his wife's sister's husband's uncle, hailed him joyfully.

"I cannot stay. I have waited long enough," muttered the donkey rider, in agitation. "Allah knows they may be already at my house, clasping my doorposts, needing my protection. I am old and have no stomach for the fray. Yet they went off bravely, that handful against a whole city. I was proud of their friendship though I slipped away. No doubt but that they have slain the Frank and all belonging to him, and have destroyed his house with fire. They come from wilds wherein vengeance is a sacred right

—as it should be, O my son—as it should be. They know not the law of this city which takes no count of religious motives. They will flee from the punishment to my house, and I must be there to shield them if I can."

"Was the riot then so serious, O my uncle? They spoke of it as a jest."

"Hadst thou seen their faces, heard their heartsome shouts as I did, thou wouldst never ask—'was it serious?'"

"Alas, for their wickedness. Very surely they are the worst of men. May Allah destroy the house of every one of them."

The fellâh contradicted Zeyd hotly: "Nay, may Allah prosper them. Art thou, then, also their enemy? Blessed guests have they been to our village. The fame of them has made us respected in all the neighborhood. They are good—the best possible—to their friends. What matter though they be bad to their enemies? Can all men use the same eyes? May Allah preserve them. In thy grace, O my dear!"

Pressed by the old man's heels, the donkey started, its shod hoofs waking echoes in that deep-walled place.

Zeyd followed, in search of the Sheykh Shems-ud-dìn, for whose safety he grew anxious. Talking of danger and punishment had brought into the foreground of his remembrance details which had failed to impress him at the time—in particular, the company of soldiers which had passed him by the city gate, and the confusion in the Frank's mad speech of Shems-ud-dìn with the Circassians. Apprehensions, spurred by indigestion of the various insults he had been forced to stomach, made his soul groan within him. At unawares he ran instead of walked—a strange sight in the city at high noon.

At length he stopped to inquire of a group of good Muslims standing gossiping before a cobbler's stall, whether anyone had seen the Sheykh Shems-ud-dìn and his unmistakable adherents. The men turned from their questioner to glance meaningly one at another. The cobbler it was who answered.

"W' Allah!" he exclaimed, pausing, needle in air, from his sewing at a certain slipper. "Go and ask at the Mehkemeh. A hundred Muslimûn are shut in there, and they say the English consul is judging them in place of our rightful Câdi. Ah, those Franks are devils. There is no end to their enormities. And our lords, who suffer them, are little better."

Zeyd stayed to hear no more. He ran on, panting, with misty eyes. Upon the fastened door of the courthouse a crowd pressed, enjoying a grievous outcry from within.

" Ha, they beat the malefactors. That is good," said a Nazarene to his neighbor. " He knows his business, this English consul."

Zeyd thundered in vain at the door. None opened, and the crowd jeered at him. With heart near to breaking, he gave up the attempt and ran headlong toward the Haràm. A great pulse throbbed in his brain, seeming the pulse of the whole world, for every object of his gaze beat with it.

The aged Mahmûd Ali, Chief of the Learned in the Holy City, was coming out of the Mosque El Aksa on the arm of a young disciple—his senile blindness doubled for the moment by the sudden sunlight dropped on him like a dazzling veil—when Zeyd, the son of Abbâs, fell groveling at his feet.

" Who is it, O my son? " quavered the sheykh, much alarmed; for he could not discern the form of the suppliant whether of man or beast.

" It is some mad derwìsh," replied the lad supporting him.

" Nay, it is I, Zeyd, the servant of the Sheykh Shems-ud-dìn. Mad am I now, and with reason, for they kill my master."

"O Allah, is it possible? Expound the matter, O most faithful of servants."

The old man heard the story sadly to an end. Then he bade his disciple lead him beneath some trees which grew by the place of washing. There, in the shade, he sat down and, taking an inkhorn, a reed, and a leaf from his girdle, wrote hurriedly.

"Here is a word from me to the Câdi," he said to Zeyd. "This is not the first time I have had to rebuke the slaves of this Mutesarrif. They plead, and with a measure of justice, that it is hard for few to govern many without indulging the majority. None the less it is iniquitous. I here threaten him with the curse of El Islâm. I adjure him by his father's grave. His father was a good old man, a friend to me. If he remember not his father, then is he rightly accursed."

Armed with that writing, Zeyd sped across the honored pavement to where his slippers lay beside the steps; and thence to the Mehkemeh, where he arrived bathed in sweat, and mouthing oddly—a maniac to all appearance. The crowd, now much diminished, withdrew from him in alarm. His knocks on the massive door reverberated as though the hall within had been as empty as it was silent.

"Open, O sons of Eblìs. In the name of Allah.

In the name of El Islâm, open, or it shall be the worse for you." Zeyd knew not what he cried. He had forgotten dignities. What mattered anything? It was the Last Day.

At that high call, the door was opened a little. Its keepers, expecting to behold some functionary, gaped on the vision of a sweat-blind vagrant. By allowance of their stupor the wretch shot past them into the court.

"Who is this? What means this?" cried a voice of anger. Zeyd was aware confusedly of men innumerable rising from the ground with shouts and harsh laughter. In that peopled dimness he faltered, dazed and abashed. He heard the voice of the enemy, the voice of Hassan Agha, calling:

"Behold the grace of Allah. It is he, the murderer, the rightful victim, brought to us by a miracle. O Excellency, slay that wicked man and spare us."

Then, of a sudden, he espied the Sheykh Shems-ud-dìn, and it was as if a light shone upon him suddenly. With a glad cry he was going toward his master when strong arms seized and carried him, kicking, before the judge.

"Praise be to Allah! We have here the culprit —not a doubt of it. We will soon extract his confession," sighed Yûsuf Effendi, with immense relief.

CHAPTER XXVI

"No; I say no. Allah forbid so great a sin. He is a good poor man, who never wronged anyone, my friend these many days. For my sake came he to this city, mistress of wickedness; and if he have sinned herein, the blame is mine. Let me die and save him."

Shems-ud-dîn stood between Yûsuf Effendi and the helpless Zeyd, confronting the former in a posture not of suppliance. The Câdi frowned, while his eyes shifted nervously from side to side, then settled on his string of beads.

"Art possessed, old man?" he remonstrated, in a whisper. "Seest thou not it is thy chance to escape? Some one must die. Let it be this dog, who is certainly not good. It is impossible thou canst know him, call him friend. Look once more on him, I entreat thee, what a vile face is there! Thou wast deceived at the first, the hall is dim. It is not thy friend, but a villain undeserving of compassion. Let him take his wages."

"If he dies, I die with him. He is my friend, my faithful follower. See, he holds a paper crumpled in his hand. It may be a writing of importance to us. Let it be read, O Excellency. Doubtless it shall explain his presence here."

"So be it; but we waste time," said the Câdi fretfully. "I grudge every minute lest by ill-hap that Nazarene should return and end my power to befriend you."

A soldier disengaged the paper from Zeyd's hand, and passed it to the judge with a reverence. Yûsuf Effendi read it and turned to stone. His eyes bolted from their sockets. Then he made the gesture of throwing dust on his head, of rending his clothes, and bemoaned the day he was born.

"O Allah, what can be done? O Allah, pity me. Let the man go, you soldiers. It is an envoy from the illustrious Mahmûd Ali. O Lord of mercy, what shall I do, whom slay? O Almighty, appoint me some victim quickly, for the pig may return who cares not though I perish, my lord with me. Oh, Allah! Allah!"

He glanced wildly round him, as though expecting his prey, new-created, to drop from heaven. Then he hid his face in his hands and wept before all men there.

His scribe, with intent to console him, set to work to make fresh coffee.

While Yûsuf remained thus, rocked with grief; while the scribe and a humbler attendant were busy about the little brazier, and the fragrance of coffee stewing caused the prisoners and their guards to lick envious lips, the door of the hall opened once again. Yûsuf groaned and his face puckered with the peevish desperation of a child. He supposed it was the Christian pig, returned to ruin him.

"Take, read, O Yûsuf," cried a voice of triumph; when, looking up in surprise, the judge beheld Abd-ur-Rahman Bey. Still sobbing, he received a flimsy slip of paper, only to return it with a moan:

"It is in Frankish character, I cannot read it."

"If my lord the Bey will deign to pass it to me, with the Câdi's leave, I can perhaps decipher it," said the scribe, once more at his post.

The scribe read, and recognized the words for Arabic. He quickly transliterated, and handed his copy to the judge.

"Ma sh' Allah! O Allah, mercy! Have compassion! In what have I sinned that such woes are stacked upon me? I am robbed, and may not take vengeance; I give judgment, and must reverse my judgment. And all that is not enough. I myself am doomed to ruin by the Grand Wazìr. On one hand, the Grand Wazìr; on the other, the Powers of

Europe. What am I to do, whom obey? Some one must die or I am ruined. Yet all these must go free, or I die. What matter in the end? Let me die, since it is so decreed."

"Calm yourself, O my dear Yûsuf," whispered Abd-ur-Rahman at his ear. "Thy plight is by no means desperate. I see many in this court who are nothing to my uncle—inquisitives of the city who have pushed in somehow. Punish a few of them and all is said."

"But . . . O Lord! . . . is it not the hour of sunset? And the consul enjoined, 'ere sunset.'"

"Take comfort. There is yet half an hour. Let me indicate the men to thee. Those four by the door will do. They serve no purpose in the world. I have seen them often in the streets, and know their kind. Act at once and secretly. Let not my father guess thy purpose. Nay, on second thoughts, what need to act at all in person? I myself will bid the soldiers hale them forth to execution; and do thou meanwhile make thy peace with my father and all these his companions."

"May Allah reward thee, O child of my soul. Thy wit has saved my honor." In the fullness of his heart the judge embraced Abd-ur-Rahman, and kissed him on both cheeks. "One other favor I must beg of thee: let some one seek out the chancellor of the English consulate, that he may see the corpses. Bid him ask if it is the consul's desire that their heads be severed and set up in some public place for an example to other malefactors."

No sooner had Abd-ur-Rahman left his side than the Câdi stepped down off the dais. Approaching the Sheykh Shems-ud-dìn, he strove to kiss his hand, craving pardon for the indignities heaped in error on one so illustrious. His urbanity fully restored, he talked and joked lightly with the prisoners, calling them his children, his soul's dear ones, smiling lovingly upon each and all of them, even upon his two robbers. Loud swelled their praise of his magnanimity, and many were the coins thrust into the hand which he held for convenience' sake behind his back. The Sheykh Shems-ud-dìn blessed him, and made him a present on account of Zeyd. With pious eyes, Yûsuf Effendi thanked God for his mercies, and repeatedly exclaimed:

" O lucky day! "

At length Abd-ur-Rahman came back to him and whispered:

" It is finished."

" The praise to Allah. You are released, all of you; your arms are restored," cried the Câdi, with bounteous gestures. "Sin no more, I beseech you; but go your ways in peace."

"In this hour we shall set out for our own place," said Hassan Agha, when the storm of blessings had subsided. He with Shibli took a penitent leave of the Sheykh Shems-ud-dìn, who would not be prevailed on to accompany them.

The court then emptied apace.

Yûsuf bowed low before Shems-ud-dìn, who, attended by Mâs and Zeyd, yet lingered in the darkening hall. He besought him:

"Deign, O my lord, to write a little—a mere word —to the brother of thy Grace, to the august Milhem Pasha, Pillar of the Throne, that he may know I have done his bidding against all opponents. Write, I pray thee, that I would do aught imaginable to oblige his noble Excellency, that I am the humblest of his servants, that I kiss the earth between his two feet. . . . O Nâsr, bring paper, ink, and a sound reed, hither to our lord. Deign to sit down. Ennoble my name, which is Yûsuf Effendi, son to Muhammed Effendi, who was formerly Mûfti in this city. May Allah Most High reward the affability of your Mighty Reverence. My house is thy house. Truly, now is my soul between thy two hands."

Shems-ud-dìn wrote as requested, and handed the

paper to the judge, who passed it on to the scribe, who made a letter of it ready for transmission through the post.

Abd-ur-Rahman stood afar off by the wall, lurking in the background, a shadow among shadows.

CHAPTER XXVII

OUTSIDE the hall of judgment it was dusk in the streets. Men wending homeward from the place of business hurried past, a dwindling stream. Their lanterns, shining with confined rays, appeared set in the first rich bloom of night like the eyes in a peacock's tail. Shems-ud-dìn desired no lantern to guide his steps. The dogs beginning to prowl after offal might snarl at his disturbance, he feared not their spite; he cared for nothing earthly. Through a gap in the hard black roofs, the flowers of heaven shone in their pleasant field. He did not observe them, all desire of the eyes, all lust of contemplation having rest within him.

Of a sudden, in a quiet place, Zeyd plucked his robe.

"Haste, O my master; the soldiers follow us!"

"Hist!" whispered Mâs from the background. "Be silent, blockhead! It is his son who follows."

Zeyd and Mâs together shrank away into the darkness.

Confused by the touch of Zeyd, by words which

had failed to pierce his sad abstraction, and yet more by the vanishing of the disturbers ere he could ask what ailed them, Shems-ud-dìn stood still, as they had left him, looking back.

A tall shape grew out of the darkness. It loomed swiftly upon him. He heard a sobbing, felt his robe caught fast in a clutch of despair.

"Forsake me not, O my father!"

It was the voice of Abd-ur-Rahman, the one voice in all the world of power to strike him. Folding his son to his breast, the old man lifted up his voice and wept.

"Ah, have mercy, O my father! Go not now to the khan, but turn aside into this entry till I bare my soul to thee."

"Is it worth the while, O beloved? Do I not know already?" said Shems-ud-dìn; but his son's will constrained him.

In a gloom so profound that the night they had left without seemed a brightness by comparison, Abd-ur-Rahman fell at his father's feet. When the sheykh strove to raise him, he uttered cries of pain.

"Let be, O my father! First hear me to an end. When I left thee to go to my uncle, I was the child of thy training; I knew no law but that God sent, in which thou hadst instructed me; I thought that all who call themselves Muslimûn deferred to that law in conscience as in form. But when I came to Istanbûl, and beheld the grandeur of that city, with its wealth and luxury, my soul doubted, and I looked two ways; for things I had reckoned sinful were there done openly in the daylight, while men of ripe years and superior judgment smiled at my careful observances and scruples against the use of this and that. After a little, thy likeness faded from my remembrance; thy maxims sounded faint amid the voices near me.

"The precepts of my uncle Milhem were not what thine had been. He is a good man in his fashion, and was very kind to me. His wisdom, his wit in talk, compelled my admiration. The high authority I saw him wield enforced respect. Moreover, having no son of his own body, he used me as the apple of his eye. He gave me money for my pleasures, more than I had ever seen in all my life. He chose for me companions, Turks, the sons of good houses, in whose society I ate and drank of abomination."

Here a burst of sobbing broke the narrative. Abd-ur-Rahman had felt his father's hand touch his brow.

"Yet for that my uncle was not angry. He only

laughed, when I confessed to him, and bade me have a care for my health. He himself was my tutor in the science of statecraft, of which he is the greatest master. From him I learnt to separate faith and behavior, the rules of government and those from Allah Most High. He placed me for a while at the customhouse, and when I had there learnt all that he wished me to learn from the conduct of the officials, he brought me into the employment of a certain wazìr, his friend. Everywhere I saw the needy turned away, while he who owned fine clothes and brought a gift in his hand secured an audience. Hence I contracted a loathing for the poor and miserable, and would never be seen in the company of a man ill-clad.

" From the closet of that wazìr I passed to the military service, in which I served but two months before the influence of my uncle procured my appointment to this garrison as a yezbashi. At the same time I received from the bounty of our Sultàn the style and dignity of Bey.

" In the parting audience my uncle informed me that he would no longer push my fortunes so openly, for fear of jealousies, but that I must make my own way on from the start he had given me. He would make me an allowance of money, which he named and I thought most handsome. Then came his last word of advice. It was to associate only with those who could further my career. He said, laughing, that he was afraid lest my father's son should waste time in the profitless frequentation of learned madmen, in relieving the wants of scabby beggars, who said never 'The Lord reward thee.' He need not have thus adjured me, for already I was the son of his teaching.

"So it came to pass, O my father, that when I came to this city, and found myself a personage courted and admired, I forbore to think on the little place of my birth, or on the friends of my youth, but made all my endeavor to appear the greatest possible, vaunting my high lineage and powerful connections. I sent no word unto thee, O my father, nor let anyone suspect thy presence upon earth. I even told a comrade, who inquired of me somewhat straitly, that I was an orphan, and that my father had been a great statesman on the pattern of my uncle Milhem."

A deep groan from the mouth of the passage caused Abd-ur-Rahman to cease speaking and start to his feet.

"Some one listens. May his house be destroyed!"

"Who is out there?" called Shems-ud-dìn; and the voice of Zeyd made answer:

"It is I, O my master, and with me Mâs the black."

"O insolence! May their fathers perish!" cried Abd-ur-Rahman.

"Nay, curse them not, my son. They are folk of our own house. In my distress, when thou and Shibli and all others left me, this Zeyd was hands and feet and ears and eyes to me. Mâs thou knowest of old; I have no need to tell thee who he is. Continue, O my soul!"

"When I received the letter warning of thy coming, which reached me in the same hour when thou shouldst arrive, I knew not what countenance to adopt. Indeed my surprise was great, for I had not written to thee, and who, I wondered, could have informed thee of my existence in El Cûds? One half of me yearned for thy blessing, while the other hnng back for fear lest by thy means some of my pretensions should be belied.

"When I beheld thee riding in so strange-looking a company, when I found thee resolute to pursue thy dealings with the Frank physician, I determined thenceforth to visit thee only in secret, and to refute every rumor of our relationship which might get abroad. Thanks to the garrulity of Hassan Agha, I was driven thrice to contradict that kind of rumor."

The narrator paused, sobbing. Again a hollow groan from the mouth of the tunnel made him wince. But he soon recovered enough force to proceed in a broken voice:

" O my father, what is left to tell? Thou knowest the end of the story, how the shock of thy captivity drove out the devil which had so long possessed me; how I strove, tardily, to repair my fault. Now see, I am the dust before thee. My companions, for whose sake I sinned, now turn from me with sneers and cutting taunts. I am become unclean in their sight.

" And now, O my father, learn my firm resolve. I will at once resign my high position and the favor of my uncle, and return with thee to our little town in the wilds, there to end my days in thy peace and in the way of the upright."

" God is Most Great! God is Most Merciful! Unto God the praise! " cried Mâs and Zeyd together from the night without.

" I approve not at all," said Shems-ud-dìn gently, yet with decision, " unless on one condition: that thou remain first a full three months at thy post. If, when that term shall have expired, thy desire be not altered, then come to us; and may Allah grant thee of His blessings! "

"But . . . O Lord!" moaned Abd-ur-Rahman, in anguish. "My companions—all my acquaintance spurn me. How can I endure for three months the scorn of all around me?"

"The scorn will not long survive its cause. And if some things I have heard are true, thou art not all contemptible, my son. Thou art called a zealous, a competent, and a clever officer; and, moreover, I hear it said that thou alone of all thy kind hast been known to refuse a bribe."

"The praise in that is not mine. It belongs, under Allah, to my uncle Milhem, who keeps me so well provided that I require not the gifts of any man. But, O my father! ask me not to endure for three months the sneer of my companions."

"I ask no less, my son. Be brave, O beloved! Consent to reap the harvest of thy sin; so shall it be expiated before Allah, whose wrath is more to be feared than my pain or the looks of thy companions. To-morrow thou wilt present me to the Mutesarrif, to the Chief of the Soldiers, and to all thy friends; and I shall contrive to let fall a word or two to lighten thy offense. Fear not that I shall bring shame or ridicule upon thee. My speech is not that of the fellâh or the muleteer. Afterwards I, in my turn, will present thee to the Chief of the Learned, whose blessing shall sustain thee through the trial. Thy mistake has been always to shun the society of the devout and studious. It is the mistake of my brother Milhem. . . . Now walk with me to the khan."

"Nay, I beseech thee! I have wept much; I would avoid the stare of strangers."

"I say not, enter with me; but bear me company as far as to the door."

The street seemed light as they came forth to it. Great stars throbbed overhead in a tranquil sky, but the grudging house shapes and frequent arches allowed but a glimpse of them. Mâs stalked in front and Zeyd behind, to kick off the dogs which soon formed a barking phalanx in their wake. Shems-ud-dìn held his son's hand in a tight clasp. At the entrance of the khan, he embraced him and let him go.

Then, having watched him depart, he caused Mâs to fetch a lantern and light him up a dark and broken stair to the roof of the hostelry, whence he could view the perfect flower of night and drink its fragrance.

The city slept around him. Except for light here and there in some upper chamber, for the shapen Dome of the Rock and a few minarets, he might have thought it an outcrop of black rock on the face of the hills. Far away to the eastward, across a gulf, appeared the rampart of his own land, vague and dreamy beneath the stars.

Peace fell about him like a pleasant rain. To-morrow he would go hand in hand with his long-lost son. To-morrow, for the last time, he would visit the grave of Alia. To-morrow, ere the sunset, he would take leave of the wicked city never to return. If Allah willed.

Alia was dead, his blindness gone. Once more he could see clearly the right way. Once more he enjoyed access to the mercy of the Most High.

CHAPTER XXVIII

THE year's last rain had fallen and the power of the summer sun was fresh on all the land. With thanks to Allah, the little party of travelers approached the region of great trees in the highland beyond Es-Salt. Mâs, walking beside the litter which contained Fatmeh, wiped his face with his hand repeatedly and shook off the drops thus reaped upon the ground.

"It is hot, O mother of stale delights," he observed friendly. "How fares it with thee inside there?"

"I stifle—I expire," moaned Fatmeh.

"Take heart, O waning moon! The shade is at hand. Already I can see one bûtm tree—a black head like mine above the hill. But shade is the parent of flies, winged devils. Mules stung by them wax restless. Thy charms will be sorely shaken."

"O Lord, have mercy! Am I not dead already?"

Mâs grinned and brought his goad to bear upon

the leading mule, which had stopped in a vain endeavor to bite its flank.

They were engaged in climbing the brow of a ridge by a path embarrassed with loose stones and occasional smooth rocks, treacherous to the hoofs. Shems-ud-dìn led the way upon his old white horse, whose tail kept swishing. He was followed by Zeyd, the son of Abbâs, a deplorable figure surmounting the last of asses. At the crown of the ascent the sheykh drew rein, allowing Zeyd to come up beside him.

" Praise to Allah! " he exclaimed, with hand shading his eyes.

Before them upon the sun-bleached slopes grew many trees, of dark foliage which looked rusty as compared with its own rich shadow.

" Praise to Allah! " echoed Zeyd, and therewith groaned, for the hour of parting was come.

At the foremost knot of trees a halt was made; the litter was set down, and the beasts took their ease in battle with the flies. Fatmeh stepped forth from her prison, strictly veiled, and sat down on the farther side of the trunks from that where her lord reclined. Zeyd lay down before the sheykh and ground his forehead in the mast from those trees. He wept:

"O dear lord! All my life shall I thank Allah for the memory of thee. Hereafter, when thou art dead and thy remains are covered with a white tomb, a wely where good men pause to pray, Zeyd will be thy pilgrim yearly. Now, after an hour or two, if God will, I shall see again my own house, my woman, and all belonging to me. By means of this ass, which the owner would not receive again, I travel comfortably. My soul will rejoice in the home-coming. Yet shall I never forget thee, O my guide. Till the Last Day I am the better for thee. May Allah reward thee for thy mercy toward me—thou high and learned, I the meanest in the land."

"O kindest, O best, O most patient of all men living," cried Shems-ud-dìn, striving to raise him.

But Zeyd clove to the dust, praying:

"Bless me, O light from Allah, before I go. A long, a learned blessing, O my master."

Shems-ud-dìn blessed him then at great length. Knowing the weakness of his poor disciple, he used to indulge it words of poetical and learned use which, for Zeyd, fell straight from heaven.

"O my eyes! O too great glory! O my soul," gasped the fellâh, moaning and wriggling in the depth of enjoyment.

At the close of the benediction, Mâs, who stood

beating off flies from the horse of Shems-ud-dìn, cried:

"O Zeyd, thou art blest indeed. I behold that blessing upon thee, a robe of purple embroidered with gold and jewelry. Henceforth thou art not like the rest of us."

Sobbing, speechless for beatitude, Zeyd struggled to his knees. He seized the sheykh's hand and, carrying it to his lips, rained passionate kisses upon it. Then, starting up, he ran to his donkey, bestrode the same, and, plying his stick, shambled off through the grove.

Shems-ud-dìn, as he watched Zeyd's form recede, now blooming in a sun ray, now fading in dense shadow, was not distressed. Time was when he would have sorrowed thus to part with the kindest of creatures. But now he saw men only as the sun sees them, while loving them for the love of God who made them.

Attendant on the beasts, Mâs had wandered to a farther group of trees, beneath which was some growth of herbage.

Over Shems-ud-dìn's head the peep of sky through the branches made separate sapphires set in ebonwork. His eyes uplifted in dreamy contemplation, he did not see Fatmeh creeping toward him round the ancient tree trunk. Only when she took his hand and pressed it to her forehead did he wake to her presence with him.

"What ails thee, woman?" he asked in dismay.

"O hard of heart! O cruel!" she whimpered. "Art thou not lord of me? Has my fancy ever strayed from thy goodliness to desire another's? Now Alia is dead, what am I? The women at the spring will mock me, saying, 'O thing despised, alone in his house, yet unembraced.' O my dear lord, O tree of sweet fruit shading me, could I tell when I joined thy harìm, to wait upon thy daughter, that by so doing I should render my widowhood eternal? I knew thou hadst no other, save me and that very old one who is since dead. . . . Let not the offense which I committed at that other tree stand ever in thy sight against me. May Allah blast that other till the Last Day. Died not my soul beneath its branches? But this is a good tree, of shade most pleasant. Ah, put me not away, O lord of justice."

Slowly the import of her blubbering reached Shems-ud-dìn's intelligence; and he saw plainly how, immersed in selfish grief, he had dealt harshly by his servant. Her desires were natural and legitimate. She was now alone in his house. He sought no other woman.

" So be it," he said. " Very kind hast thou been to me through this time of trouble. When the days of my grief are accomplished, if Allah spares us, thou shalt have thy will."

The creature's gladness seemed excessive to one for whom all things were now equal under heaven.

In the wide archway of his own house, overlooking the small white city which had been his care so many years, the minaret which he had caused to be built, and the yellow hills rolling to violet in the distance, Shems-ud-dìn sat on a morning and wrote to his brother Milhem. Behind him, in the shadow, knelt Mâs employed in trimming the lamps of the house, shaking one after another to be sure it had oil enough. The sheykh paused often before recharging his reed to gaze out over the sun-baked land and smile, part ruefully.

" After inquiry touching thy illustrious health, I submit to thee, O my dear brother, that my son Abd-ur-Rahman does, upon mature reflection, elect to retire to a private station and has returned to this little city, to the house of me his father; that he entreats thy pardon for a defection which must bear the look of ingratitude; but that, in excuse, he has not the strength of thee, O my brother, to escape corruption in a path so full of temptations. Forget not, O my dear, how his childhood was spent in a quiet place, among simple folk, far from all those seductions which spring from too much luxury and the intercourse with foreigners and men unsteadfast in the faith.

"Notwithstanding, I will not hide from thee my own lively pleasure in this end to his deliberations, which appears to me the right one in the sight of Allah.

"Furthermore, let me thank thee once again for thy gracious intervention when Allah willed that I should be accused falsely in El Cûds, whither I went last spring, on an evil prompting, to subject my beloved daughter, then very ill, to the treatment of a Frank physician, in whose house she died very peacefully, the praise to Allah. Though sad for the loss of my daughter, and more for the inordinate affection my soul bore her, which conscience tells was the cause of that loss, I am not unhappy. Thanks to Allah! Here I am surrounded by friends who wish me well. A woman, long a servant in my house and attendant on my little Alia, now tends to the comfort of my age, and lavishes on me the endearments for which her sort were created. Hassan Agha, our old acquaintance, was felled from his horse and wounded recently in a conflict with certain of the Bedû who, harboring a grudge against him for some wrong he did to them in El Cûds, have harried us these three months past—against all precedent, for their time of sojourn here is the winter—but now seem gone from the land, for which we praise Allah. As for Hassan, thy bounteous grant of rifles and powder has done much to reconcile him to my son, with whom he quarreled in El Cûds. All my neighbors, alike Arab and Circassian, honored my son with a great reception on his arrival yesterday in the morning.

" And now, O my brother, once more I beseech thee to forgive thy brother and the son of thy brother, who are both very sensible of meriting thy most just displeasure. And May Allah preserve thee always."

This letter, when folded and sealed, was intrusted to the soldier servant of Abd-ur-Rahman, who was obliged to set out that day on his return to El Cûds.

In less than a month it was answered. A trooper from the garrison of Esh-Shâm, calling God and his horse to witness that he had ridden day and night without a halt, delivered the missive to Shems-ud-dìn as he sat in the entry of his house toward sunset. With the usual courtesies, it ran:

"I have received thy honored letter, and though I grieve much for the loss of a youth whom I had come to regard as my son (a thing I could never procure of my own body, though I have tried many women and begotten at divers times no less than sixteen daughters, if I count aright, so that I have come to hate girl children as a deception, and utterly fail to comprehend thy infatuation for that girl who died), yet I will not disguise from thee that the withdrawal of the young one has done me good in my position. It is but policy in the sovereign to look askance on the posterity of men of note; and that custom of the Turks is wise by which honors descend not from father to son. The eyes of many in high places regarded with disfavor my fondness for Abd-ur-Rahman; but now, an old man without a sequel, I arouse no hatred, only expectations. What am I, thus lonely, but a kind of eunuch, a natural and unenviable appanage of sovereignty.

"I rejoice to learn in what love and esteem thou art held by all who know thee. As for me, I am beset with fears and hostile ambitions. Never in my life have I inspired sincere affection, save only in thee, O my brother. By Allah, the image of your little town rises tempting now in my mind, though in the days I was condemned to sojourn there I deemed it Jehennûm. It is because of our love, O my brother, for the sake of our parting there at daybreak among the rocks, that the thought of it now allures me. I am old and thou art old, but if it is the will of Allah that I fall some day from use, as may well betide—should my life then be spared and exile satisfy the lust of my enemies—I shall choose for place of banishment thy little town beneath the hill of ruins, and count it bliss to end my days at peace in the house of my brother."

When Shems-ud-dìn looked up from the writing, he was blind with crowded visions of a bygone day. Out of the evening calm he looked and saw the vanity of man's endeavor, from least to greatest, upon the earth, and how it floats on God's mercy as a boat on the mighty deep. And he cried from his soul:

"Allah is greatest!"

(1)

THE END